Praise for *The Gyamkian Revolution*

"*The Gyamkian Revolution* offers a powerful vision for the Gitxsan people, as the road opens clearly before the next generation. This writing not only revitalizes legal knowledge, but actively prepares Gitxsan youth to walk forward with confidence and pride."

—*Xsiwis (Dr. M. Jane Smith) Wils 'Wii K'aax, Lax Gibuu, Gitxsan Education Scholar, Language Teacher, and author of* Returning the Feathers

"This book is a profound and generous gift of collective self-understanding offered to Gitxsan Wilpsters by Gitxsan Wilpsters."

—*Lisa Guenther, Queen's University*

"*The Gyamkian Revolution* summarizes and narrates the present 21st century struggles for Indigenous freedom and resurgence into a context building on Gitxsan tradition and governance. In this book, the next generation of Gitxsan leaders articulate a pathway to the future that has global relevance—an achievement of monumental proportions and relevant reading to all."

—*Tero Mustonen, Snowchange Cooperative (Finland), Winner of the 2023 Goldman Prize*

"*The Gyamkian Revolution* powerfully asserts Gitxsan values in the face of histories that have been hostile their continuance. Sutherland-Wilson and Wright show both the strength of the traditions they call on and how those traditions might be reanimated to face new challenges. It can be hard to imagine how to end settler colonialism, but to me, this work looks like one way to begin an ending."

—*Jill Stauffer, Haverford College*

THE GYAMKIAN REVOLUTION

The Gyamkian Revolution

30 29 28 27 26 1 2 3 4 5

University of Manitoba Press
Winnipeg, Manitoba, Canada
Treaty 1 Territory
uofmpress.ca

For EU product safety concerns please contact Mare Nostrum Group B.V., Mauritskade 21D, 1091 GC Amsterdam, The Netherlands, gpsr@mare-nostrum.co.uk.

Cataloguing data available from Library and Archives Canada
ISBN 978-177284-154-1 (PAPER)
ISBN 978-177284-156-5 (PDF)
ISBN 9781-77284-157-2 (EPUB)
ISBN 978-177284-155-8 (BOUND)

Cover design by David Drummond
Cover art by Kolin Wilson-Sutherland
Interior design by Karen Armstrong

The University of Manitoba Press acknowledges the financial support for its publication program provided by the Government of Canada through the Canada Book Fund, the Canada Council for the Arts, the Manitoba Department of Sport, Culture, and Heritage, the Manitoba Arts Council, and the Manitoba Book Publishing Tax Credit.

Funded by the Government of Canada | Canada

CERTIFIED CANADIAN PUBLISHER

THE GYAMKIAN REVOLUTION

The Wilpsters
of Git'tsim'gedimgyat and Git'luuhl'um'hetxwit

UMP
University of Manitoba Press

A NOTE ON AUTHORSHIP

University of Manitoba Press respects the Gitxsan legal protocols of authorship attribution in accordance with House family intellectual property laws. This work contests colonial categories of authorship and gives due credit to the owners and decision makers of the oral histories rematriated and represented in the book for the well-being of the next generation.

CONTENTS

FOREWORD

by Sim'oogit Hawaaw (Marilyn Wright), on behalf of the Git'tsim'gedimgyat family

I rise today as Sim'oogit Hawaaw.

I come from the House of Git'tsim'gedimgyat, a wolf clan family of Anspayaxw. My wilksiwitxw is the fireweed House of Git'luuhl'um'hetxwit also from Anspayaxw. My grandfather, the late Sim'oogit Tsi'basaa (Stanley Wilson), and my grandmother, Sim'oogit Hawaaw (Alice Wilson), married on 10 October 1941, the last arranged marriage between our two House families.

Sim'oogit Tsi'basaa and Hawaaw raised me as a daughter in the laws and feast protocols of our people. Through their teachings, I was prepared to carry this name, and today I uphold it with the daxgyet, the governing powers of my House.

This book reflects the life and future of Git'tsim'gedimgyat and Git'luuhl'um'hetxwit, two Houses from the sixty-plus matrilineal Gitxsan families that comprise the Gitxsan legal order. It was prepared following our legal protocols, with extensive discussions and selection of the spokespeople responsible for sharing our ancestral knowledge: my nephew, Hooxi'i, Kolin Sutherland-Wilson, a land defender and the grandchild of Sim'oogit Tsi'basaa, and my daughter, Karissa Wright, a land defender and the matriarch in training to be my successor. Their work continues our inter-Wilp alliance, a sacred bond of many generations.

The strength of this book is not in two voices alone, but in the work of each person in our House families who offered their talents to this project. It carries the Wilp wisdom of our ancestors, grandparents, parents, children, and grandchildren who have kept our laws alive in the face of genocide. We are here to stay, unceded and unsurrendered.

This work is inspired by the land. It calls us back to our fishing site Gwinoop, to the berry patches of Xsan Seegit, and to every place where our people have fished and given thanks on the waters. *The Gyamkian Revolution* reminds us that our laws come from taking care of each other on our Lax'yip.

The next generation of Gitxsan are called to uphold the ayookxwm gwelx ye'enst, the law of leaving behind a healthy House family and territory for those who come after us. The histories and ideas shared here offer insights into how we may work together with greater vision and unity. It honours our people and welcomes all into a revolution of the heart and spirit.

INTRODUCTION

LESSONS FROM STAND WITH WET'SUWET'EN

by Kolin Wilson-Sutherland and Karissa Wright

> It won't stop as long as the RCMP and [Coastal GasLink] are on Wet'suwet'en territory without their consent.
>
> —*Kolin Sutherland-Wilson, Yintah, 2024*

> This is just the beginning . . . you woke all these warriors up!
>
> —*Karissa Wright, Yintah, 2024*

More than five years have passed since we stood with our Wet'suwet'en family against the documented state and corporate violence connected to the unauthorized Coastal GasLink project.[1] In solidarity with the Wet'suwet'en and the Tyendinaga Mohawk land defenders on the east coast, we helped shut down Canada and the British Columbia Legislature. What did we learn from this flashpoint experience? We learned that extraction projects like Coastal GasLink and the zombie pipeline project known as the Prince Rupert Gas Transmission, resurrected in the spring of 2024 by the Nisga'a Lisims government and the Texas-based company Western LNG LLC, will continue unabated unless we stand together as united House families. We learned that despite the power imbalances we face, and the tactics that seek to divide and conquer our people—tactics financed by U.S. billionaires who hire militarized private security to ensure their projects are driven through our lands—we remain unwavering in our stand. From Maas Gwitgunuxws (Teresa Brown)'s no-kill zone dog sanctuary, Wilp Aasosxw, located on the Gitluudaahlxw territory where the Prince Rupert Gas Transmission pipeline is planned but will not cut through, to the rise of the Lax'yip Firekeepers—a Gitxsan inter-Wilp youth movement dedicated to stewarding our Gitxsan territories and defending them against further unauthorized extraction—we have learned how everyday resurgence continues in creative and intergenerational ways.[2] We have learned about the intimate depths and widths and heights of our love for the land and all life that calls it home. It is irrepressible and expansive, this love, and it can never be extinguished.

Speaking from these depths and as beloved cousins from the wolf and fireweed House families of Git'tsim'gedimgyat and Git'luuhl'um'hetxwit, we hope to give present and future generations an understanding that serves the continued work of rebuilding this sense of compassion, belonging, and legal order on our territories among our families.

After shutting down Canada in 2020, we continued to learn and grow in our Gitxsan legal education and training at a pace uncompromised by the culture of speed and advancement in the academy.[3] In the learning tempo set by our own Houses—where Gitxsan law truly lives and breathes—one of our peoples' epic discoveries, long before Copernicus, was how our legal order and cosmology orbited around the Sun. In the winter of 2022, Nii'lax Aks (Denzel Sutherland-Wilson) brought to our attention *Men of M'deek and Wars of M'deek*, a rare book coming out of the Tsimshian village of Kitselas authored by our fireweed relative Neas-D-Hok (Walter Wright). In the mid-1930s, Neas-D-Hok transcribed his oral histories with the help of his good friend Will Robinson.[4] "Laws they had," Neas-D-Hok says of his ancestors, "but these were few; laws framed by Wise Men who watched the face of nature; who pondered long on the workings of Gyamk, the Sun God who lived in the Sky City of Laha; laws that were made as they watched the cause and effect work out their ends in the lives of men."[5] These words set us on a search for Gyamk.

From records of oral accounts taken in the early twentieth century by our wolf clan relative Gusgai'in (William Beynon) and his colleague Marius Barbeau, we found the origin story of Gyamk to be a story of cosmic compassion entering our consciousness during a time of genocide some 6,000 years ago.[6] Based on these records, as well as later accounts provided by Gitxsan family leaders, it is said that the village of Kunradal raided and killed the people of Keemelay.[7] Only a grandmother and her granddaughter survived. Ska'wo, the granddaughter, had been confined to a retreat house as part of her ha'wehbxws, a puberty rite overseen by her grandmother, 'Nii Ts'iits Ska'wo. To rebuild their family, the matriarchs decided to create out of devastating loss.[8] It is said 'Nii Ts'iits Ska'wo first sought out support from the order of sbil naxnox, the spirit powers in the land, water, and sky:

> "How bitter my complaint, how utter my despair, O Sun, Moon, Spirits that travel on high night and day! Must you see Keemelay lie in its ashes, and let its hunting-grounds be ransacked? Must there be no law in the land, no posterity to my [grand]daughter [Ska'wo], no posterity for a morrow and a new awakening? Must there be only an end, O Powers above algyah, algyah, algyah!"[9]
>
> O Powers above speak, speak, speak!
>
> "'Naa dim ant naks hlguuhlxwy'a Ska'wo?' she calls out, again and again."[10]
>
> Who will marry my granddaughter Ska'wo?

Eventually, one of Gyamk's descendants, Gyetm Maxmagii, a Rainbow Being, comes down from the sky to offer partnership. After testing Gyetm Maxmagii's fitness, 'Nii Ts'iits Ska'wo approves their marriage. Ska'wo then travels with Gyetm Maxmagii to an alternate universe. There, through the power of light rays, she gives birth to several babies. At dawn, Gyamk bathes each of his grandchildren in a milky creek called Maudeks. He gently stretches their limbs in the water, causing rapid growth "like the fireweeds in the spring of the year."[11] After training each according to their gifts and talents, Gyamk sends Ska'wo and her children back to Earth with the vocation of rebuilding their legal order and thriving as families once again on their territories. From this matriarchal journey through the cosmos unfolds the fireweed clan history of the Gitxsan, the people of the Skeena River.

To help us rebuild in our time, we follow the legacy of our matriarchal ancestors and seek out the Sun once more for a new awakening. To this end, we find Gyamk speaking in the surviving Gitxsanimx̲ language.[12] As when our jiitzs' and yee'es, our grannies and grandpas, begin to sweat on the bleachers while watching a summer soccer game or when in winter one takes a sip of their morning coffee and burns their tongue, both may exclaim: "Ugh, gal gyamk!"[13] Too hot. Or more profoundly so, when one of our loved ones returned home to Anspayaxw this past summer with her young nieces and reconnected with relatives they hadn't seen in years. "Gyamk goot'y," she tells us, was the only expression that conveyed how the homecoming had her heart so "full of warmth and happiness."[14] These everyday Gitxsanimx̱ terms suggest an enduring presence that is at once formidable and essential to life. Gyamk is our genius loci, the guardian spirit of our power and place in the universe.

This raises the question, what happened to Gyamk? Why are there relatively few references in the recorded oral histories? More recently, why was a Gyamkian cosmology not a part of the official submissions in the *Delgamuukw–Gisday'wa* land and jurisdiction case brought forward by the Gitxsan and Wet'suwet'en people in the 1980s?[15] From our research and reflections to date, we suggest Gyamk underwent a molten transformation in the ears and tongues of early missionaries. These folks heavily relied on language to convert coastal peoples to Christianity in the nineteenth century.[16] Gyamk melted into a monotheistic concept of Father- or Chief-in-the-Sky—Sim'oogit Laxha in the Gitxsanimx̱ language. The term then became a synonym for the Christian God. We see this semantic slippage occurring even in Neas-D-Hok, Gusg̱ai'in, and Barbeau's respective accounts of Gyamk and in various later accounts of spirituality by Gitxsan people in the generations before us.[17]

Instigating a Gyamkian Revolution today therefore entails playing the Raven, as it were, by stealing back the discourse on the Sun.[18] This work involves using our eyes and ears to watch out and listen for more glimmers of Gyamk coming off the page or out of the mouths of our people. In this way, we aim to translate and further the molten transformation in a manner that ensures the continuance of our solar-powered system of law and governance so that in the days ahead we will have more than a half-baked cosmology scorched by settler-colonization. As Madiigam Gyamk (Neil J. Sterritt) put it, "Now, in the aftermath, we need to rekindle a new vision and revive broadly shared values that will allow future generations to achieve the outcomes our elders fought for."[19] Heeding this call, our book—as a family labour of love—can be thought of as a grassroots guide back to Gyamk, which is to say a journey back to the bare bones of our legal culture.

In Part 1, The Wilpster Uprising, we explore the Wilp (House), the Pdeek (Clan), the Lax'yip (Territory), and the Yukxw (Feast). In Chapter 1, we look at the historic child naming system practised by all House families. A baby name was and remains a birthright. It nourishes a sense of personal identity as Wilpsters; that is, as people who belong to a Wilp, a loving family network kept alive through the mother's line. We lay out a way of restoring our child naming system to promote inclusive citizenship. In Chapter 2, we study how clan governance serves to foster mutual aid among House families across long distances and how we may continue to practise clan principles to help each other learn and grow within the Gitxsan legal order. In Chapter 3, we go on to look at how our ancestral territories were established in response to a major migration of refugees some four millennia ago, from the ancient city of Temlaxam to the surrounding villages along the Skeena. We suggest this hospitality is the basis for taking care of our territories and protecting them against Crown infringements. Finally, in Chapter 4, we consider pole-raising feasts and how these feasts may help us reconnect with our House histories and exercise effective governance moving forward.

In Part 2, Gyamkian Formations, we reimagine our Gyamkian cosmology for the times. In Chapter 5, we highlight how bathing, fasting, and harvesting bush medicine on our territories are practices connected to our Gyamkian origins and continue to offer us the strength and insight necessary to help us through shared difficulties. In Chapter 6, we engage Albert Einstein's notion of "cosmic religion" to democratically interpret Gyamk from a number of spiritual, scientific, and pop cultural perspectives that amount to an equation that balances the work of taking care of ourselves with taking care of each other.[20] In Chapter 7, we offer a strength-based model of our wilpsta talents that calls for an annual awards show that confers the Order of Gyamk on those doing outstanding work in the Gitxsan humanities, sciences, and civic engagements.

In Part 3, Git'Fit Training, we detail our democratic culture that nourishes those talents and regards all Gitxsan as fit to lead. We all have a duty to learn and teach.[21] In Chapter 8, we look at the leadership training tradition expressed by the hereditary chiefs Spookw and Hanamuxw at a 1945 pole-raising feast in the village of Gitsegukla. Finally, in Chapter 9 we set out a vision of peaceful living inspired by the gawagaani tradition of eagle down taught by our House matriarchs and grandmothers, Xhliimlaxha (Martha Brown) and Antgulilbix (Mary Johnson). We apply their legal principles to respond to the Missing and Murdered Indigenous Women and Girls (MMIWG)'s calls to justice aimed at ending child abuse, gender-based violence, sexual violence, and lateral violence in our communities.[22] As one of our family leaders 'Wii Muk'willixw (Art Wilson) teaches us, "we have to deal with these issues or the cycles will never be broken."[23]

In the Epilogue, we heed the voice of Madiigam Gyamk once again and call for unity across generational, House, clan, and village lines so that we may be one big family under a Sun that is truly ours.

We hope this journey is of value to all readers. To fellow Gitxsan and our coastal neighbours, may you find a language and a conceptual toolkit that aids in reincarnating a sense of who you are. To students, scholars, and the broader public, we hope our collaborative cousin research and writing reveals to you the relational and intellectual foundation of Indigenous legal orders in Canada.[24] The Gitxsan basis is the warmth of Gyamk that calls us to step out of our confines once and for all and step into the light of a new day. Whether we are Gitxsan, Canadian, or some other kind of cousin, *The Gyamkian Revolution* is an invitation to travel through the cosmos together and return to our family and friends as whole and lawful people.

PART 1

THE WILPSTER UPRISING

1

WILP/ HOUSE

Like I told before, when a child got his or her first name, and then later on he got another name, and that's how they rise up to be a Dax gyat, rise up and up until it gets to be a higher chief, so he has power of all the names and all the territory and fishing sites and all the mountains.

—*Antgulilbix*[1]

Scholars of Gitxsan law and history have long debated the meaning of "uprising."[2] It is typically used to denote conflicts between Gitxsan people and early settlers over jurisdiction and territories. As articulated by Antgulilbix (Mary Johnson) during the *Delgamuukw-Gisday'wa* trial, a Wilpster Uprising is about empowering each Gitxsan person with a name, a place, and a calling to grow and give back to their House. In this chapter, we use the term to speak of the productive work of resolving internal conflicts and confusions over House names. A Wilpster Uprising begins with the child's first name and culminates in the dax-gyat, the dignified power, held by our family leaders and their Houses.

Before going further into the details of this Wilpster Uprising, it is helpful to make clear what we think it means and what it does not mean to be Gitxsan. Historically, the Gitxsan, Tsimshian, and Nisga'a trace their origins to the great migration out of the ancient city of Temlaxam some four millennia ago.[3] With the city ruined by a snowstorm, the Temlaxam refugees settled in the smaller villages along the Skeena and Nass Rivers. *Git* is the plural of *gyat*, meaning the people, and *xsan* derives from the words *xsi* (river) and *yenk* (mould). Antgulilbix recalls a time when the Skeena was so full of fish that the surface of the water would be covered by mould from the fish oil. Some would make fun of the Gitxsan as people of the mouldy river, which is why it may have been changed at some point to mean "misty" river, derived from the components *git* (people), *xsi* (river), and *ye'en* (mist). Following Antgulilbix, we believe the original meaning is a beautiful thing. To be Gitxsan is to be connected to the territories surrounding this once wealthy waterway.

With the arrival of ethnographers, colonial administrators, and missionaries, the Gitxsan and Nisga'a were homogenized as Tsimshian for much of the nineteenth and twentieth centuries.[4] The Indian Act further divided us into bands and sequestered us on reserves near our seasonal village sites. In place of the Simgigyet, the matrilineal leaders of each House, the Indian Act privileged patrilineal descent and granted authority to elected chief and council. In place of the Lax'yip, the Houses' ancestral territories stretching 33,000 square kilometres, the chief and council allotted small parcels of lands reserved for Indians totalling 90.385 square kilometres among the six Gitxsan reserves today. As such, Indian Act band membership constructed and continues to impose a relationship of dependency on the state-funded band office, causing division on the reserves as families fight over band control while "on reserve" and "off reserve" members vie for federal funding and services. From a Gitxsan perspective, the Indian Act was set up to eliminate our sense of ourselves as Wilpsters, bringing our lives and our territories into the claws of the Crown. A system that aims to sever us from our rich inheritance of rising House names by reducing us to a registry number. A lawful Gitxsan is not a number.

Contrary to ethnographic and Indian Act definitions of who we are, publicly available oral histories like Neas-D-Hok's reveal that coastal peoples organized first as families and clans, often basing their collective identity on a naxnox spirit power they encountered on the land. In the case of Neas-D-Hok's House, this was the m'deek, or supernatural grizzly bear, that attacked Temlaxam after the people had forgotten to respect the trout. Such naxnox experiences were often commemorated in chiefly names, songs, and on a House's ayuks, crest designs, to remind the family of what they endured together and to always uphold the Law of Gyamk.[5] Continuing in the freshwater flow of this tradition, the Gyamkian Revolution is about returning to our House families and clans for true and lasting identity and governance.

This return transcends time and space, for the House is a bond rooted in ancient lineage and territory that ventures to branch out today across nuclear family units, time zones, and settler states. It is a bond nourished and encumbered by Canada Post letters, Zoom meetings, long-distance phone calls, Facebook chats, and visits back home, at the Feast Hall, in the city, hospital, prison, halfway house, college campus, on the streets, territories, and blockades, and wherever else Wilpsters might be at any given moment in their lifetimes. In this way, the House remains a travelling group of persevering people who remind each other of their shared history and life callings. At its best, the House is a transgenerational movement that treks through the full catastrophe of living.[6] This messy work of being-with, caring-for, and thinking-through with one's own House on the manifold matters of life is what it has always meant to be a lawful Gitxsan.

The Child Naming System

Gitxsan child rights activist and scholar Cindy Blackstock calls us to ask, "What does a healthy Gitxsan family and child look like?"[7] In our view, a healthy House family is one in which each Wilpster feels a sense of warmth, belonging, and meaningful direction across the lifespan. This sense begins with the baby name.

As taught to us by Hanamuxw (Don Ryan), the baby name is actually a reincarnational one.[8] It is the name we are given at birth and it is the name that we return to upon our death. As Antgulilbix told the court, the rising up in power over the House's territories, from the waters to the mountains, starts with the child's first name. A baby name is a birth right. It announces to all that this little one belongs to *this* House and is dearly valued by all in the family. What's more, it invites the youngest to contribute to the House. A baby name followed by a feast seating name, a wing-chief name, and perhaps even the head chief name, among other honours. After attaining all of these distinctions, the highest chiefs humbly return to their baby names. We call this growth and uprising in one's roles and responsibilities, validated by a variety of House names throughout one's lifetime, our Gyamkian citizenship. It is cosmic in scope and compassionate in depth. For instance, the head chief name held by Martha Brown, X̲hliimlax̲ha, translates as

"Walks Across the Sky." As Xhliimlaxha, she spoke of how "it's in the traditional law that the families help each other out."[9] This is the basis of Gyamkian citizenship.

As it stands today, this rolling out of names in relation to various rites of passage and developmental stages is more theoretical than real. From what we see and hear from our families, the problem is deeply felt. Genocide has fragmented our knowledge base and the transmission of House names, which has, in turn, undermined our lawful sense of ourselves. There are misunderstandings and confusions galore about names that need to be clarified in order for a Wilpster Uprising to emerge once more in the twenty-first century and beyond.

To support this effort, in the remainder of the chapter we draw on a few publicly available sources that detail how House families innovated and conferred baby names. We hope that these examples provide the clarity and creative licence for House families to rebuild the naming system as practised by our ancestors.

We start with Antgulilbix herself. In her expert witness testimony, she teaches about her own baby name, Gwalx luu wan, which means "the bear cubs stay in their den during wintertime." She explains that it is a type of wam sii halayt, a new dancer name. "The Gitksan custom," she says, "is to give the baby the first name and they call it sii halayt. It's not a great big yukxw. They said it's a Feast just among the village. They got two names at that time. . . . My other name is Sagayt 'na lo'ixsxw," which is an ear-piercing name that translates to "they all come out dancing together."[10] While both names belong to her mother's House, she explains how the first name involved her father who "comes from a Wolf tribe and the wolves were there . . . [at the feast]." She later states that the name "connects with the crest of the father."[11] Here she is referring to her father's pdeek, or clan, the wolves, specifically the Hawaaw family. Her father's House displays a white grizzly bear on one of its carved poles.[12] She further explains that if her father was from one of the three other clans—the frogs, fireweed, or eagles—this would have resulted in an entirely different baby name. Importantly, Antgulilbix affirms that this child naming system is about receiving the daxgyet of the father's House and clan, and this applies to all Gitxsan people: "When the wolves call out the name of the child and they mention their crest so that means they put their power on the name, on the new name, and it still is today from—on every Gitksan people."[13]

In the scholarly literature, the anthropologist Wilson Duff elaborates on Antgulilbix's account of the Wilpster Uprising. He explains that baby names were selected from the stock of names owned by the child's matrilineal House, yet also identified the child's father's House. He provides an example out of Gitsegukla. In that village, there is a girl's name, ni'gamks, that belongs to one of the frog Houses. It means "on sunshine." If the girl's father belonged to the fireweed (also known as the killer whale) clan, then Duff suggests the name could possibly be expanded into "sunshine glinting on the wet dorsal of the emerging Killer Whale."[14] Alternatively, if the girl's father belonged to the eagle clan, then the name could translate as "sunshine glinting on the white head of the Eagle."[15] As Duff copied and transcribed several baby names as part of his research, he recognized how each "conjures a striking image of the crest animal. . . . Each conveys its image by means of a clever and economical use of language, and each (I am sure, although I am not a speaker of Tsimshian) rolls pleasingly off the tongue. In short each may be described as a sort of one-line poem, and consequently this type of name may be considered as one of the art forms of the Tsimshian [*sic*]."[16]

The Gitanyow account of the naming protocols for children further clarifies the Wilpster Uprising. In 1959, the House families from Gitanyow village published a book to educate the public about their histories, territories, and laws.[17] The text explains how the naming protocols for children are organized into four ceremonies. The process begins with a meeting "to which all the villagers are invited as witnesses." Then the House leaders "call out the name of the child and the father presents gifts to all those who called out the name." The child's name is known as na-muk. The subsequent protocols are reserved for children who will be trained for the chiefly names owned by their House.

In the second ceremony, boys have their ears pierced by their aunties while girls have a hole put through the lower part of their lip. At this stage, the children acquire another name; for boys it is known as shak-gwee-qus, and for girls it is called ark-gahs. The third ceremony is dedicated to training the children in the songs and dances owned by their House. The hereditary leaders use rattles and perform dances, and with the motions of their arms "throw their power into the children." They then place the headdress on the child, covered in eagle down, a symbol of peace. This ceremony is known as sii halayt.

In the final ceremony, another feast is held where hereditary leaders confer a "higher title" on the child. At this point, children hold the "right to enter the feast-house and can receive gifts." Upon the death of a House leader, they are qualified to carry on that person's daxgyet, their power and responsibilities to the House and its territories. When this occurs, the youth are required to distribute their wealth among the other House leaders in the village. This grants the youth the right to attend their feasts. The same protocol applies to feasts hosted in another village. The ability to contribute to each feast is a sign of the youth's desire to "step up until he reaches the top." Consistent contributions over time build up the youth's reputation as the successor to the highest names in the House.[18]

This protocol summary helps us make sense of why Antgulilbix received two names at her birth. The first is what all children receive, and the second, the ear-piercing name, signalled that she would be trained for the highest names in her House. At the age of twelve, upon the death of her great-great-grandmother, she was thus prepared to take up the power of her first wam sim'oogit name, Anhalagyax.[19] She also received other names throughout her life. For instance, at her marriage feast, her grandmother's sister Lucy Tait gave her a divorce name, Gwiis logam phlo'on, which translates as *old white sea otter blanket*.[20] It was a name once held by her auntie Kate Hakst. Later in life, her other grandmother Edith Gawa gave her the name Xsim Wilaat, a wam gyat name that means *Lady Echo*.[21] When her uncle George Williams died, her auntie Lucy Tait gave her the hla ga kaaxhl sim'oogit (wing-chief) name of Guxws didalkxw, once held by her uncle Donald Mowatt. At her divorce feast, she received the previously mentioned divorce name along with Hamiyaahl hloxs, which means *the sun is always thankful*.[22] Finally, at the age of seventy-three, she took up her auntie Emily Latz's power as Antgulilbix, one of the highest names in her House, and defended her family's territories at the *Delgamuukw-Gisday'wa* trial.[23] In total, her lifelong Gyamkian citizenship was marked by eight distinct names that began and ended with Gwalx luu wan, *the bear cubs stay in their den during wintertime*.

Child Naming Today

These examples offer guidance on how we may revitalize the child naming system today. Historically, child names were given at birth at village-level feasts where the family leaders of the mother's and father's Houses called out and conferred the names. As the fireweed matriarch Gwaans (Olive Ryan) clarified at trial, "That's what they do. The Gitksan always do that when a child was born and they gather, the father's side. And they come and they hold the baby. They call it iinoowhlxw."[24] Secondly, while these names are owned by matrilineal Houses they cannot be created solely by them. Rather, baby names are cocreated with the child's father's House and clan because the names invoke patrilineal ayuks, crest designs. This means each House family needs to collaborate with the child's father's side to provide the name reflective of the child's full lineage.

Here we should pause to identify some of the assumptions in this knowledge exchange between Houses. For one, there are heterosexual norms in the Gitxsanimx̱ language of lineage, "mother's House" and "father's House." Research by Gyooksg̱an (Val Napoleon) indicates the House family system relied on heterosexual relationships for its organization and continuance. As such, the kinship terms do not reflect the full range of gender identities and sexual orientations held by Gitxsan people today. What's more, there is an absence of gender and sexual orientation diversity in recorded oral histories. Gyooksg̱an therefore advocates for the underlying kinship principles to be applied in ways that affirm the human rights and agency of all Gitxsan people.[25] Informed by her research, it is important to state that our use of such terms is focused on the underlying legal principles of caring for children (in this case, protection of identity) and remains inclusive and respectful of the gender identities and sexual orientations of all Gitxsan. Moving forward, we also encourage House families to make ample space for discussions about gender and sexual orientation and how this relates to kinship terms. As Gitxsan scholar Gina Mowatt eloquently puts it: "Women, queer, trans and 2spirit Indigenous people are othered within liberatory frameworks that are allegedly made for us. . . . This issue does not necessarily call for adding Indigenous women, queer, trans, 2spirit people atop these foundations, but for a complete disavowal of Indigenous theories and frameworks that assume a Native subject as cis-hetero man."[26] Two-Spirit, lesbian, gay, bisexual, transgender, queer, questioning, intersex, asexual, and/or gender diverse or nonbinary voices and perspectives, among others, need to be heard and their paradigms placed at the centre of how we govern moving forward. Such dialogues would help examine the gender assumptions in historical baby names owned by each House and the development of gender-inclusive baby names.

The child naming system also assumes a baby has both a Gitxsan mother and Gitxsan father from different clans. Historically, when Gitxsan people married their neighbours, such as the Wet'suwet'en or Nisga'a, they provided dual clan citizenship to their children through adoption practices. For instance, Madiigam Gyamk (Neil J. Sterritt) was born to a Gitxsan father and non-Gitxsan mother. His mother was thus adopted into the fireweed House of Gitluudaahlxw, and this made him a member of that House. Conversely, where children are born to a Gitxsan mother and non-Gitxsan father, they could be adopted into the mother's father's House or the maternal grandfather's House. In situations where there are two Gitxsan parents who belong to the same clan, what is known as gaats or in-clan marriage, adoption is also the legitimate practice. Historically, gaats has been deemed unlawful because it deprived Gitxsan children of dual clan citizenship, breaking down the relational basis of Gitxsan legal order. To correct this, children have been adopted into either their mother's or father's House, which remains a legitimate option today.[27]

Another dilemma to child naming is that many Gitxsan children are in Crown custody. Blackstock speaks of how the overrepresentation of First Nation children in care is a continuation of colonial violence: "And, to give you a sense of the scale of it just for on-reserve, between 1989 and 2012, we've known that First Nations kids are 12 times more likely to go into child welfare care, primarily driven by neglect, primarily driven by poverty, substance misuse and by poor housing."[28] We will address the issue of child abuse further in Chapter 9. Here we will say that the state agencies, Indigenous organizations, and families involved with Gitxsan children in care need to work closely with House families to ensure they receive a baby name as a human right. To this end, the Truth and Reconciliation Commission's Call to Action no. 17 recommends that "all levels of government . . . enable residential school Survivors and their families to reclaim names changed by the residential school system by waiving administrative costs of five years for the name-change process and the revision of official identity documents."[29]

Another challenge caused by colonization is that many House families do not have a record of their historic baby names, nor do they have a working knowledge of their specific crests (beyond the clan crests of frog, fireweed, wolf, and eagle). This is where interdisciplinary research on our own Houses, or what we call wilpography, becomes vital to the rebuilding process. In this respect, the repatriation of each House's intellectual property compiled during the *Delgamuukw-Gisday'wa* case is key to a Wilpster Uprising. At the end of his book *Mapping My Way Home*, Madiigam Gyamk notes that the University of British Columbia continues to hold all of the original documents developed during the case. He calls for a library and archive centre to be established on our territories so that all Gitxsan and Wet'suwet'en peoples, including high school students and young professionals, may learn first-hand about "their rich and remarkable history and laws."[30] Some of these documents include genealogical charts and lists of names owned by House families that would be helpful to the cocreation of children's names. Adults may even do research to develop a name for themselves and share this with their respective Houses. Research and dialogue among House families *is* the collaborative work of law that makes name reclamation an empowering practice.

Our suggestions have been premised on the revitalization of the historic cross-clan naming system. While we believe it is a worthwhile legal tradition to restore, we are not suggesting it is the only way that House families may innovate and bestow baby names on their loved ones. Each House is unique and free to create anew. To this end, we believe there are enduring aspects of the historic naming system that can be integrated into a number of new child naming methods. What is critical is that however methods are developed, the process be transparent, inclusive, and remain centred on creating a sense of warmth and belonging for all Wilpsters to grow and contribute. It is also key for House naming systems to acknowledge that the nameless status of its members have been caused by colonialism. The root cause is political, not individual. This means we are responsible for learning and rebuilding together without blame or shame.

One way House families may respectfully redress the matter is by planning and hosting village-level feasts with the sole purpose of conferring children names to all, from the newborns to the eldest. There are several merits to this approach. Firstly, it would not single out the nameless status of particular individuals. Secondly, it would remedy the current problematic trend we see of in-House fighting over a limited number of feast seating and chiefly names. If we do not create and confer baby names to address this shortage, we will continue to see the tendency of certain branches within a House holding onto names and conferring names to their immediate and youngest descendants, names that may have specific responsibilities and be held by adult members in other branches of the same House. Thirdly, child naming feasts would raise awareness and dialogue about Gyamkian citizenship as an expansive growth experience that involves the receiving and giving of names throughout one's lifetime, set precedent for other House families to do likewise, and diversify the kinds of feasts we organize and host moving forward. Finally, when we reflect upon the creative element of children's names—the poetic dwelling in the Gitxsanimx̱ language, the ear and lip piercings, the handling of musical instruments like rattles, the performance of songs and dances, and placing the eagle down headdress regalia on children, among other arts of engagement[31]—we imagine an opportunity for House families to be alive to the possibilities of newness. Child naming feasts are occasions to reincarnate our legal culture in a fashion that welcomes the next generation into the House as uprising Wilpsters.

2

PDEEK/ CLAN

That's our Indian law. We help each other in the Wolf Clan.

—*X̲hliimlax̲ha*[1]

As we've seen with the making of baby names in the last chapter, the Gitxsan legal order relies on many House families coming together from different clans to help each other. This hospitality went overlooked by early twentieth-century anthropologists who claimed the clan system held "no important function other than the regulation of spouse selection."[2] Based on evidence collected over the past thirty years, the late anthropologist David Graeber and archaeologist David Wengrow have shown how clan governance systems are actually a sophisticated form of "long-distance organization" that granted people the freedom of mobility and safety on each continent and even across continents.[3] People who would otherwise be divided by regional and language differences were identified by clan crests and welcomed into new territories as relatives.

We have both experienced this hospitality in our personal journeys. In our land defence work and travels up the northwest coast and interior, from Kitkatla to Hagwilget, we have been embraced as brothers and sisters by fireweed and wolf clan Houses of the Tsimshian and Wet'suwet'en peoples. We mention these anecdotes to reveal how clan systems have not been completely destroyed by settler-colonization. Far from it. They continue to operate across long distances and to shape our lives in meaningful ways.

Our aim in the next two chapters is to expand our understanding of pdeek governance by bringing clan relationships into the light of Gyamk. Just as Gyamk helped our matriarchal ancestors 'Nii Ts'iits Ska'wo and Ska'wo in a time of genocide, in this chapter we ask: What role do clans have in helping us rebuild after settler-colonial devastation?

Gisk'aast. Lax See'l-Ganada. Lax Gibuu. Lax Skiik.

The Fireweed. The Frogs. The Wolves. The Eagles.

These four comprise the clans of the Gitxsan. Clans are kin, the matrilineal and patrilineal relations that connect us in durable relationships tested over millennia. The ancestors of the fireweed and frogs come out of the ancient city of Temlaxam that ran on both sides of the Skeena River, stretching to the upstream end close to Anspayaxw, and downstream far below the Bulkley and Skeena junction and as far as Carnaby.[4] The earliest ancestors of the wolves and eagles originate from Laxwiiyip, a settlement that coexisted with Temlaxam in an open tundra area at the headwaters of the Stikine, Nass, and Skeena on Tahltan territory near Mount Edziza. They eventually moved down the Stikine River to the coast where they encountered the Tlingit-speaking eagle clan.[5] With the great Temlaxam migration and the formation of smaller villages surrounding the ancient city, these four clans aligned and arranged themselves in a sustainable fashion that has allowed their descendants to experience the twenty-first century.

Today, each Gitxsan village is populated by a particular mix of clans. In the western downriver villages, Gitsegukla has fireweed and frog Houses; Gitanyow is home to wolves and frogs; eagle, wolf, and frog Houses populate Kitwanga. Upriver to the east, the historic northern villages of Kaldo'o and Kisga̲'ga̲'as were home to several House families that migrated south over the last century to the current villages of Anspayaxw, Sikedakhl, and Gitanmaax now populated by wolf, frog, and fireweed clan families. Throughout history, many families branched off and joined other Houses and village sites for a variety of reasons, including matrimonial and spiritual disagreements, epidemics that decimated House numbers, and natural disasters that destroyed settlements like Temlaxam.[6] These migration patterns reveal the perennial realities of conflict within and between Houses, the adaptability of Houses, and the abiding hospitality of clans to warmly accept new Houses into their territories as kin.

In Gitxsan legal thought, pdeek governance is based on a sgano, a weave, a solid fabric that makes this warm-hearted Gyamkian hospitality possible.[7] It extends out through the mother's lineage in what is known as the wilnadaahl, closely related clan Houses. It also moves through the father's wilnadaahl. From the perspective of the child, the wilnadaahl is known as the wilksiwitxw. Together, the wilnadaahl and wilksiwitxw connect House families together along clan lines to ensure the growth of the next generation. This sgano serves to support individual House families in time of need, witness and confirm their crests and territories, and take care of all life on those territories. In what follows, we clarify the sgano at the same time as we identify what hinders a climate of Gyamkian hospitality today and how we might reincarnate it anew.

Wilnadaahl: "One Big Family"

Wilnadaahl is one of those mobile Gitxsan concepts that eludes precise definition, for it is shaped by the situations courageously faced by clan-affiliated House families in solidarity.[8] For instance, there are occasions when host speakers in the Feast Hall identify their wilnadaahl as all of the Houses of their clan who attended and helped with their feast. On other occasions, a speaker may acknowledge the clan Houses living in a particular village at a specific time as wilnadaahl. It may also be used to refer to a smaller circle of Houses who can recount oral histories of ancient origins and migrations taken as a family. In this respect, it may bespeak Houses that have joined together in the past or that temporarily remain together as a sto'wilp, a larger integrated House family.

We offer here our respective Houses as an example. It was customary for a House to take on new names and identities as a family, beyond its head chief name. Tsi'basaa and Antgulilbix are fireweed family leaders with historic roots in Anspayaxw that go back to the time of Temlaxam. Together with many other chiefs on their table today, their House is known as Git'luuhl'um'hetxwit, the people from the House that stands in front. They have a long-standing history and relationship with fireweed House of Gitluudaahlxw. It is true to say, then, that Antgulilbix, Tsi'basaa, and Gitluudaahlxw are wilnadaahl. Similarly, when Hawaaw, Gwaxskiik, and Skabek̲ broke from the House of Malii in Gitanyow and settled in Anspayaxw, they became collectively known as the House of

Hagwenoodet, the fugitives. By 1920, Woosimlaxha (Jimmy Williams) speaks of how the Hawaaw, Gwaxskiik, and Skabek along with their close wolf relatives 'Wii Muugilsxw and Xsaxgyoo became known as the House of T'sømgedømgét (contemporary Gitxsanimx spelling: Git'tsim'gedimgyat). Here is how wolf clan chief Gusga'in (William Beynon) transcribes it:

> VI house of hawá.'o
>
> ———
>
> —house name:
> t̓sømgedømgét
> into/fasten/man
> salmon and downstream
> It is explained by the myth; one dragging the other on top of (see myth of house).[9]

The "salmon and downstream" notes appear to be making reference to the part of the adaawk in which one of our first ancestors, a gambler who took the name Gwaxskiik, is said to have been fastened in a canoe by his rival and sent downstream to his demise. It makes sense that this would be the House name in light of Beynon's notes at the end of the adaawk: "This narrative is the adaorh [adaawk] of that name. The informant [Jimmy Williams] learned it from his own father who was the head of the house. He heard it many times. It was recited at the feast when the name of Gwarhskyaek or Hawaoo was assumed."[10] Hawaaw, Skabek, Gwaxskiik, 'Wii Muugulsxw, and Xsaxgyoo are closely related, wilnadaahl collectively known as the House of Git'tsim'gedimgyat. Given the range of possible meanings of the term, we regard the wilnadaahl as a moving affirmation of kin. "One big family," as our father and great-uncle 'Wii Muk'willixw (Art Wilson) has taught us.

One of the main responsibilities of House leaders is to offer big family support to their wilnadaahl in times of need and crisis. That is the context in which Xhliimlaxha (Martha Brown) spoke of Indian law as this law of helping each other in the wolf clan. In her commissioned evidence for *Delgamuukw-Gisday'wa*, she details how she made a hawal, a financial contribution, to Matilda Morrison's death feast in September 1985.[11] Matilda Morrison belonged to the wolf House of Eelast. While this House is not in Martha Brown's immediate wilnadaahl, her hawal contribution signalled that her legal obligation to help extends to all wolf Houses in the village. "It's in the traditional law that the families help each other out," she explains. Following the same law, Antgulilbix (Mary Johnson) helped her Gitluudaahlxw family in the 1980s when it was experiencing a population collapse. To support the House, she organized the adoption of several members from the related fireweed Houses of Anspayaxw. At trial, Gitluudaahlxw (Pete Muldoe) testified to her leadership: "Mary Johnson was on that too, but sometimes we happened to be there but she was the one that adopted them."[12]

It is now our turn to build on the legacies of our House matriarchs by keeping this formal helping tradition alive. Following X̲hliimlax̲ha, we need to continue to offer financial aid when called upon by our wilnadaahl to support those facing hardships. We also need to coordinate adoptions within our wilnadaahl to ensure the continuance of each House family and to provide each Wilpster with the full benefits of dual clan citizenship. Both of these obligations require Houses to have access to their ancestral territories, as it is the resources on the Lax'yip that has sustained each House family and that has made wealth distribution across Houses and at feasts possible.

To this end, the territorial boundaries for each House need to be clarified, as some misunderstandings have resulted from the *Delgamuukw-Gisday'wa* court action. For trial purposes, it was common for one family leader of a House to speak on behalf of other House families within its wilnadaahl. Antgulilbix spoke on behalf of Tsi'basaa (Stanley Wilson), for instance, while X̲hliimlax̲ha spoke on behalf of Hawaaw (Alice Wilson), 'Wii Muk'willixw (Art Wilson), and X̲saxgyoo (Gertie Sterritt). This representation of the wilnadaahl, however, meant that only some House territories within the wilnadaahl were featured on the official maps.

For instance, in the wilnadaahl of X̲hliimlax̲ha, 'Wii Muugulsxw, Hawaaw, and X̲saxgyoo, only the territories of X̲hliimlax̲ha and 'Wii Muugulsxw are identified on the maps, despite the fact that Hawaaw has its own distinct territory located on the east side of the Kispiox River, known as Xsan Seegit, on the 17 mile point in the Kispiox Valley.[13] As Hawaaw (Alice Wilson) stated in a sworn affidavit: "The boundary is near the bridge at 17 mile on the Kispiox River, there used to be a village there a long time ago. The boundary is on the east side of the river and it goes up as far as Marty Allen's ranch, his ranch is on my territory."[14]

Since the court case, the incomplete maps have been used by the Gitxsan Treaty Society and Gitxsan Development Corporation to inform negotiations and to finalize deals between a handful of family leaders and Crown corporations interested in extracting resources. The problem is that the selective naming on maps has resulted in some chiefs signing deals on behalf of other Houses within their wilnadaahl without the prior consultation or informed consent of those families. In our view, signing agreements in this manner is an infringement of the law upheld by X̲hliimlax̲ha and Antgulilbix. Resource extraction projects brokered under these conditions disregard our law of consent.[15] It also creates an inhospitable wilnadaahl climate and a breakdown in trust and legitimacy of the Simgigyet, House family leaders.[16]

In speaking this truth, we need to be understanding of all sides impacted by this situation and offer practical ways for the wilnadaahl to grow in mutual trust once more. Firstly, we acknowledge the difficult position our family leaders find themselves in after a long-fought court battle that was intended to have our legal order recognized by the Crown. Many in our eldest generation have endured the residential and day school genocides and are the hardest hit by intergenerational traumas. They are now in their seventies and eighties, and we imagine it has felt like a war of attrition. When the Crown now comes to the table with promises and offers, it is understandable that they feel these have been earned by the court action championed by the Houses they represent. These agreements may even be viewed as signs of reconciliation. More cynically, some consultation and compensation is better than none, the logic may also go.

We must keep in mind too that family leaders are up against a state-funded and police-backed Crown that has far more resources and enforcements to infringe and leverage deals as it pleases, including with band councils that further undermine clan governance. Given these political and capitalist pressures, along with the high levels of poverty in the area, we empathize with the House family leaders who have been implicated in closed-door corporate transactions. As the Gitxsan political scientist Morgan Mowatt reminds us: "The Gitxsan have a saying, 'Always leave one mistake on the blanket.' It is a part of the Gitxsan worldview that we do not feign perfection. Mistake making and repair is of great importance to authority-making through relationship. For the Gitxsan this means the work is never done, that there is always more to learn and ways to do better."[17]

Like the Indian Act system itself, the whole post–*Delgamuukw-Gisday'wa* situation is ultimately the result of the Crown's failure to reckon with our full jurisdiction over our territories. As such, it is not so much a dishonour of Gitxsan law as it is a deeper dishonour of the Crown.

So how do we move forward as wilnadaahl? We might begin with Gyamkian hospitality, a warm Wilpster climate that springs to life a new surge of learning and upholding our legal order in and outside of the Feast Hall. A warm Wilpster climate that fosters intellectual freedom in which everyone has a right to raise questions and to express their views and concerns with their leaders. A warm Wilpster climate that promotes political freedom in which everyone has a democratic right to open deliberations and a say in all House decisions. Finally, a warm Wilpster climate that encourages multijurisdictional freedom in which everyone has a right to study, interpret, and argue the meaning of ayookxw niyee, Gitxsan law, its relation to other legal orders, and to appeal a House decision when it is believed to infringe Gitxsan legal principles.

Gyamkian hospitality makes ample space for these inalienable Wilpster rights, for they are about helping and protecting the most vulnerable in the House—those without names, without dual clan citizenship, without full mobility, or without full intellectual capacity, among other disabilities. Ensuring these rights are upheld in all wilnadaahl discussions and decisions is just as much about helping each other as contributing hawal at a death feast or repopulating a House on the brink of collapse. It is the true Indian law, the ayookxw niyee, our matriarchs defended in court as our rightful inheritance.

Wilksiwitxw: "Coming Out to Help"

Wilksiwitxw can be translated as "coming out" and refers to a child's connection to their father's wilnadaahl.[18] Wilksiwitxw are the House families closely related to the father's House who play a co-parenting role in each child's life, teaching them about their territories, histories, and the House relationships of their wilnadaahl. This training entails providing the children access to the father's House territories and limited privileges to use its resources for the duration of their father's lifetime, a practice known as amnigwoot.[19] The wilksiwitxw also provide guidance and support over the children's entire lifespan, including taking care of all end-of-life expenses.

When we turn our attention to the father's side today, we do so with an interest in how the wilksiwitxw can come out to help foster Gyamkian hospitality. In her community-based research, Gyooksgan identifies the wilnadaahl, wilksiwitxw, and other Houses in each village as providing a "second layer of reciprocal accountability" around a House's decision making.[20] Her findings correct the commonly held misconception that a House is entirely autonomous in its decisions, allowing for no external House intervention whatsoever. To be clear, a House *does* have authority over its intellectual property (i.e., its crests, names, oral histories) and territories. However, when decisions impact other Houses and territories or when disputes arise and House leaders have vested interests in particular outcomes, this is when trusted Wilpsters of the wilnadaahl and the wilksiwitxw are consulted and come out to help assess and resolve the matter with a greater degree of distance from the dispute and with the larger public interest in mind. When we take into account how current disputes over names and territories are complicated by Crown and corporate third-party interests, we believe the "coming out to help" clan custom urgently needs to be mobilized here in order to protect broader Gitxsan interests.

Of course, this is easier said than done, for the reality is that the roles and responsibilities of the wilnadaahl and wilksiwitxw have been damaged under conditions of genocide. We are living in a time in which our people may not know their House or clan; or if they do, may not have knowledge of their House's surviving intellectual property; or if they do, may not have stepped foot on their House territories; or if they have, may not know their House's sgano relationships to other House families and their territories. This is all by Crown design.

In response to this level of breakdown, and in keeping with the mobile meanings of these kinship terms, a special onus lands on all of us to help out. At this point in our history, we believe it is integral to reincarnate the spirit and intent of wilnadaahl and wilksiwitxw in relation to ourselves and whoever else may need our help. We propose an added reincarnational layer of reciprocal accountability to the sgano weave that allows us to be one big family under the Sun in ways not limited by immediate House, clan, and village markers (although these helping connections may align with preexisting lineage ties). This reincarnational layer extends to all our cousins and allies, Indigenous and settler alike, who sincerely seek to learn how to live and relate within our Gitxsan legal order.

Moreover, by enacting this extra layer of responsibility we may create the occasions to speak about the historic wilnadaahl and wilksiwitxw work of helping each other and its impetus for us to care for our own people. The virtue of this approach is that it can be taken up by anyone, for it is all about how we treat each other on the daily.

As an invitation into this reincarnational spirit of being one big family, we briefly detail three pdeek principles we can follow in our personal lives as a means of strengthening and extending the sgano, the solid fabric that weaves and holds us all together. As cousins, we are grateful to have experienced much healing and growth by following these principles in our many conversations over the years.

1. Gya'am niin/I see you. Often said at the end of our conversation, gyam'am niin translates as "I see you" and honours the spirit of wilksiwitxw. It sees the Wilpster as a whole person, as they are in any given moment. The gift here is in giving the time and space to validate another's life experience—the good and not so good, the beautiful and disagreeable, the serious and humorous, and all shades in between. Gya'am niin helps us to ask: What are our loved ones going through? What are their emotional realities? Gya'am niin is about attending wholeheartedly to a situation faced by someone we love. It's about using our ears and listening with compassion. All Gitxsan law turns on this one witnessing act.

2. Nax' niin/I hear you. Nax' niin is about letting our family know we get it, we understand their perspective and concerns. Many of us find ourselves working in organizations or engaging with invalidating systems where our points of view and experiences are often ignored, distorted, or otherwise undermined by people in positions of authority who have no understanding of Gitxsan law and legal order. There is power in relating to each other as Wilpsters. The recognition that we have a voice in our House

families is itself a revolutionary act that can awaken us out of the confines and categories of settler-colonialism.

3. T'ooyaxs'y niin/I thank you. Just as important as it is to see and hear our family as they are, it is vital to express gratitude for the opportunity to be a part of their lives in this way. T'ooyaxs'y niin is an expression of praise that speaks to the level of trust it takes to share our lives and House concerns with each other. It calls us to hold our conversations in full confidence. T'ooyaxs'y niin celebrates the wonders of knowing each other as kin. With gratitude in our hearts, no one is taken for granted.

Gya'am niin, nax' niin, t'ooyaxs'y niin. I see you, I hear you, I thank you. These expressions convey the relational building blocks of Gitxsan law. They convey the underlying principles of wilnadaahl and wilksiwitxw within and across lines of lineage and location. They remain an ever-present choice in how we relate to each other. Before we can be this to anyone else, we have to be wilnadaahl and wilksiwitxw to ourselves, giving much warmth and gratitude to our spirits for doing their best to learn ayookxw niyee and helping us find our true voice that deserves to be heard.

By tracing the sgano, the solid fabric of our clan relationships, we hope to have expanded our sense of what kin-based governance is really about. Pdeek principles reach far beyond the regulation of marriage. Although clan governance did and continues to inform matrimonial matters, these choices were and are grounded in the deeper function of providing pdeek provisions between House families. Pdeek principles are long-distance affairs.

We circle back to our own Houses to illustrate this point. The House families of Tsi'basaa and Hawaaw enjoy a matrimonial alliance that goes back at least five generations, with the last marriage occurring on 10 October 1941 between Tsi'basaa (Stanley Wilson) and Hawaaw (Alice Wilson). Their union followed previous chiefly marriages arranged by their Houses to ensure all their descendants inherited the wealth of their shared territories and the intellectual and social enrichment that comes with long-standing, cross-clan relationships. In this sense, pdeek principles did not "regulate" matrimonial relations so much as they nourished cross-clan generosity that transcended the lives of two individuals and the respective interests of two House families.

In this chapter, we have sought to offer ways of carrying on the legacy of the Tsi'basaa-Hawaaw matrimonial alliance and the work of our wilnadaahl matriarchs X̲hliimlax̲ha and Antgulilbix. To be Gitxsan is to be a part of an ancient alliance of clans. What we learn from our own wolf-fireweed House union is that we need to arrange our relations in ways that ensure present and future generations grow to know each other and our neighbours as one big family under the Sun. This is the genius of Gyamkian hospitality, the warm-heartedness our ancestors weaved along the northwest coast for thousands of years. How much farther can we weave a solid fabric across this land?

3

LAX'YIP/ TERRITORY

My great-great-grandmother lived a long time and told me everything. She said, "We're a *caring* and *sharing* people."

—Tsi'basaa, as heard by Hooxi'i on the Lax'yip in the summer of 2021

Since the onset of settler-colonization, much of the thinking about our 33,000 square kilometres of sixty-plus House territories has been understood in terms of a clash between the Gitxsan and the Crown over jurisdiction and ownership, especially so with the *Delgamuukw-Gisday'wa* case and subsequent negotiations, impact benefit agreements, blockades, and commentaries from media and scholars alike on the ongoing legal situation.[1] While it is undeniable that the House territories have been infringed and that land defence remains necessary, we believe it is just as essential to return to the underlying impetus for defending our territories in the first place. What is the Lax'yip governance system really about? When and for what purpose did our people establish it? And how does it all relate to the Law of Gyamk, the law of *caring* and *sharing*, as Tsi'basaa (Leonard Gawa) learned of it from his great-great-grandmother?

Based on the archive of oral histories, we detail the Lax'yip governance system in terms of its original purpose of providing a place and home for the scores of refugees who fled Temlaxam, the ancient city ultimately ruined by a catastrophic snowfall some 4,000 years ago. To illustrate how this upheaval was managed by the clans of surrounding villages, we share the intersecting fireweed and wolf clan journeys made by our House families from Temlaxam to our present-day territories near the village of Anspayaxw.

We then go on to critically assess the Crown's doctrine of Aboriginal title. Proclaimed in 1997 by the Supreme Court of Canada as sui generis land property rights "in a class of their own," these circumscribed rights were quickly implemented by provincial and federal agents in the Nisg̲a'a Treaty (1999). In later decisions like *Tsilhqot'in* (2014), the Supreme Court further entrenched Aboriginal title in the colonial myths of terra nullius, the doctrine of discovery, and underlying Crown title.[2] We argue that as it currently stands, Aboriginal title is an affront to the sovereignty of the Gitxsan Lax'yip governance system. Accordingly, we call for a paradigm shift from sui generis to 'wii gyamk generous, from thinking of Aboriginal title as a limited land property right to an expansive sovereign right to enact and uphold our laws on our House territories as voiced by our family leaders on day one of the Delgamuukw trial.[3] When the Crown reconciles with this paradigm, the Lax'yip governance system will have the legal protection and freedom to continue to exercise the Gyamkian generosity originally established in response to the postapocalyptic Temlaxam crisis.

Territory in the Time of Temlaxam

As the dispersal from the city of Temlaxam is estimated to have occurred about four millennia ago, what we suggest about the people's relationship to territory are reasonable inferences based on the oral histories shared at trial by fireweed matriarchs Antgulilbix (Mary Johnson) and Gwaans (Olive Ryan).[4] Their oral accounts belong to what is known in Gitxsanimx̲ as the Temlaxam adaawk.[5] They learned these histories from their wilnadaahl, including their grandmother and great-great-grandmother, respectively.[6] The pivotal events of their adaawk pertain to a series of natural disasters culminating in the people's decision to finally abandon the city.

Antgulilbix and Gwaans speak of three specific disasters. First, there is the mediik adaawk.[7] After the people of Temlaxam finished their hunting, fishing, and berry picking, it was custom for the girls to make camp at a lake at the foot of the Stekyoden Mountain. There they caught grouse and many trout. At some point, one cut out the backbone of a trout and used it "as a decoration" while singing and dancing. Seeing how beautiful she looked in the water's reflection, the girl encouraged her peers to do likewise. Members of their family would come over and watch for entertainment. After they finished camp, on their way back to Temlaxam they heard a loud noise. Suddenly, they saw tall trees being thrown about and a giant grizzly bear stomping along a stream that connected the lake to the Skeena River. The warriors were called in, but their arrows bounced off the bear and it crushed them to death, one by one. The mediik entered Temlaxam where it killed many more people before returning to the lake, where it disappeared. The disappearance suggests it was a naxnox, the power of the trout seeking revenge for being disrespected. Antgulilbix provides the following reasons for why the people continue to tell of the event: "That's why the wise elders told the young people not to play around with fish or meat or anything, because the—because the Sun God gave them food to eat and those who—just . . . they should just take enough to eat and not to play with it, that's why this tragedy happens to them."[8]

The second account details the revenge of the one-horned mountain goat.[9] According to Gwaans, young boys were throwing little goats into a fire for sport and "making fun" of them. Some of the people in Temlaxam, hunters and Elders, tried to advise the youth against this behaviour. One boy listened and took compassion, rescuing one from the fire. He placed 'mes, red ochre medicine, on its face and returned it to the mountain. The baby goat's name was 'Waak, meaning "brother." Sometime after this, the people of Temlaxam were invited by a foreign group to attend a feast. At the feast, during the opening halayt dance, the hall started to shake and quickly collapsed. The hosts of the feast were the mountain goats disguised as humans. All the Temlaxam guests fell down the mountain to their demise except for one, the young man who helped the baby goat. In its human form, 'Waak wore the red ochre face paint and provided shoes for his rescuer. He then led him safely down the mountain back to Temlaxam. The Gitxsan youth then told the elders in the city about the tragedy. Gwaans summarizes the implicit law of this adaawk, "Well, that's what they said. They don't allow us to make fun of those little, little things, the amxsiwaa [white] creature. That's what they said to . . . the young people, not to make fun of those animals, because the creator's going to get mad if you mistreat them. That's what grandmother said."[10]

The third oral history recounts the final dispersal of the people. According to Antgulilbix, it happened during the spring when the people were cooking large salmon over the fire. A little boy was given a stick of fish, and while eating it he looked up and noticed a cloud covering the Stekyoden Mountain. It had snowed, and the boy ridiculed the sky, "'What you going to do with this?' waving the little stick, 'You was snowing again.'"[11] That night the people of Temlaxam were snowed in. Over time, they ran out of wood and grew cold. One day, one of the chiefs noticed a bird with a leaf of berries in its beak sitting on the smoke hole of their house, indicating the storm had only hit the city. It was summer on the rest of the land. So the young men were called to dig through the snow. When they came out, as Antgulilbix tells it, they noticed their "land had been changed," and so "each group that understood each other . . . they follow the rest, and they went in different directions."[12]

In all three cases of Temlaxam adaawk, the disasters occurred in times of prosperity and leisure. They were preceded by the youth expressing careless attitudes towards the fish, the mountain goat, and the sky that resulted in derision and degradation. When Antgulilbix speaks of the "Sun God" and Gwaans of the "Creator" becoming heated over these instances of mistreatment, we take this to mean the Law of Gyamk—the bare-bones law of respect for all forms of life, from the salmon to the sky—had been transgressed. These transgressions of the heart are the real tragedies in the adaawk. The three accounts likely reflect a broader pattern of societal breakdown in Temlaxam. It raises the question, why did they continue to rebuild a system that did not support a sustainable legal order? In our view, it was the Temlaxam land arrangements that created surplus that lured them back. It was that singular focus on surplus accumulation that created the impediments to remembering and enacting the Law of Gyamk across generations. It took a flurry to finally break the vicious Temlaxam cycle.

Territory in the Aftermath of Temlaxam

How is it possible that people not only survived the aftermath but were able to build the basis of the Gitxsan Lax'yip governance system we know today? We argue pdeek principles played a vital role. To illustrate this, we briefly trace here the fireweed and wolf clan migrations of our

House families from the ancient city to our present-day territories surrounding the village of Anspayaxw.

We begin with the House of Git'luuhl'um'hetxwit. In her testimony, Antgulilbix relays the journey of two sisters, Sagayt ga'ak and Naga'ihl, and their younger brother, Wildim waax. They initially found refuge in the western village of Gitsegukla, among the related House of Haxbagwootxw.[13] When a famine struck the village, the siblings left, travelling on a giant log down the Gitsegukla River. They soon experienced tragedy, with Wildim waax starving to death along the way. To survive, the sisters killed a drumming grouse that landed on the mossy part of the log. Afterwards, Antgulilbix states, "they sat down and they both cried. They remember their brother that's just died and they compose a dirge song." It is at this point in the adaawk that the House shares a limx'ooy, a mourning song, to commemorate the loss of life. This event is also recorded on one of its carved poles restored in Anspayaxw in 1973. The pole features the young girl "holding the grouse with tears in her eyes."[14] The grouse itself remains a major House crest. The account continues with the sisters finding an enormous fireweed, a gil'haast, and snaring a one-horned mountain goat. These two events are also prominent crests, with the latter featuring at the top of another carved pole raised in 1916 in Anspayaxw. The sisters eventually formed a village at what is known today as Wilt gallii bax, located below Andamhl, a mountain "where the moon shines on," behind the present-day village of Sikedakhl. Wilt gallii bax remains the unceded territory of Git'luuhl'um'hetxwit. While maintaining connections to their Lax'yip, Git'luuhl'um'hetxwit was later invited by their Temlaxam sibling, Gitluudaahlxw, to move to Anspayaxw. As Antgulilbix recounts it, Gitluudaahlxw talked "things over with Tsibasaa and ask him to move up to Kispiox. Even though it's not far away, but they want to be together . . . that's the reason why our Feast House stands in front of all the houses at Kispiox, that's why our House name is Luu hlim hetxwit, that means 'Standing in front.'"[15]

For the House of Git'tsim'gedimgyat, the ancestors took a different path from Temlaxam to Anspayaxw. According to the oral history recounted by 'Wii Muugulsxw (Jonathan Johnson), Ts'iiyee was a Temlaxam warrior who fled the city with his family down the Skeena River, first turning north to the village of Gitanyow.[16] There they integrated with the wolf House of Malii. During one summer, Ts'iiyee set out alone eastward on a hunting trip. He followed a small creek that joined a river somewhat larger than the one that connects with the lake near Gitanyow. This river was filled with an abundance of salmon, so much so that they crowded one another out of the water. Ts'iiyee called the creek Tsihl'nii'din, as all the fish made him think of "fat bubbling in a pot." Eager to explore more of the area, he stayed the night. The next day, as he was making fire, he saw a man rushing at him along the narrow bar of gravel. In self-defence, he drew his club and charged at the stranger. A wrestling match ensued for some time until the stranger grunted, "I know you. Are you not Ts'iiyee, my neighbour in the days of Temlaham?" Tsi'iiyee then recognized it was Yeel', a short-tempered fellow warrior who had made the area his hiding ground. It is said that although Yeel' wanted the territory for himself, he recognized the futility of sparring over it with Tsi'iiyee, and so he offered him the river on both sides from Ts'ihl'nii'din down to Anxya'gen, which is the present-day McCully Creek to 17 mile at the head of the canyon. Ts'iiyee's territories went all across the valley, mountain to mountain, while Yeel' maintained the river from the canyon to its mouth. According to 'Wii Muugulsxw, after this land agreement was reached, Yeel', being a "big-hearted man in many ways, confessed to being lonely all these years. He said it would be good to have a neighbour, and one he had always held in respect." Thus the Temlaxam warriors stayed together many days before Ts'iiyee went back to Gitanyow and returned with his large family. "This valley," 'Wii Muugulsxw says, "has been their home ever since."[17] Today, we know Ts'iiyee as the Temlaxam ancestor to the House of X̲hliimlax̲ha, while Yeel' is considered a sibling forebear to the House of Gitluudaahlxw.[18]

Hawaaw was one of the families within the wolf House of Malii that provided Ts'iiyee and his family refuge from Temlaxam. According to the ethnographic archive, sometime after Ts'iiyee migrated to Anspayaxw, the Hawaaw family also "branched off" after matrimonial disagreements involving Malii's nephews.[19] Hawaaw along with Gwaxskiik and Skabek̲ relocated their families to Anspayaxw, likely because of their prior relationship to Ts'iiyee and his family. When the smallpox epidemic hit the village in 1862, several Houses were decimated, bringing the count in Anspayaxw down to just 225 people in 1890.[20] In response to this crisis, the Hawaaw family joined closely with Gwaxskiik, Skabek̲, 'Wii Muugilsxw, and X̲saxgyoo. Today, Hawaaw remains a leader in the House of Git'tsim'gedimgyat and continues to own and steward its fishing site, Gwin'oop, in addition to its names, crests, and unceded territories east of the Kispiox River along the 17 mile point of the Kispiox Valley, known as Xsan Seegit.

From these migrations, we may gather a few truths about the emergence of the Lax'yip governance system. The first is the important role played by the western villages of Gitsekugla and Gitanyow as first responders to the Temlaxam exiles. In these villages, it fell to the fireweed and wolf clan Houses respectively to offer safe haven. Haxbagwootxw taking care of Antgulilbix and Tsi'basaa. Yet these were only temporary abodes. The Temlaxam ancestors to Tsi'basaa and Antgulilbix went downriver while Ts'iiyee ventured eastward on foot with a warrior desire for more hunting grounds. There was from the get-go an openness towards mobility, exercised by each House as an inalienable right in order to freely meet their needs and pursue their aspirations. In the case of Tsi'basaa-Antgulilbix, we learn too how a House's territory, on which their ancient village of Wilt gallii bax was located, may be retained while relocating to a nearby village. With Hawaaw, we witness how a House can branch off and find a new home in another village and share territories with related wolf Houses.

In both instances, what ultimately draws these persevering House families into Anspayaxw is a mutual longing to be "one big family" as in the days of Temlaxam. Gitluudaahlxw wanting "to be together" with Antgulilbix and Tsi'basaa, and big-hearted Yeel' looking for company with an old friend in Ts'iiyee. In the flux and flow of these expansive movements in time and space, in the orbits and oscillations within the circulating chambers of these ancestral hearts, the Temlaxam diaspora brought about *new* House relations, *new* crests and clan alliances, *new* territories, carved poles, and villages that, far from hiding out, have rumbled up over the past three centuries to consistently help each other out against the odds and against Crown-imposed constraints. This is the Lax'yip governance system, bubbling like fat in a pot.

Territory in a Post-*Delgamuukw* Dark Age

More than twenty-five years have passed since the *Delgamuukw-Gisday'wa* case, a court action led by our House family leaders in defence of our Gitxsan territories. Initially denied by Justice McEachern in 1991, an appeal was launched in 1993 reaching the Supreme Court of

Canada. On 11 December 1997, the decision affirmed that Aboriginal title was a preexisting right that had not been extinguished by the Crown. Although falling short of a full declaration of title over our Lax'yip, the decision encouraged good faith negotiations on both sides to reconcile state law with Gitxsan and Wet'suwet'en legal orders.

To date, there has been no meaningful reconciliation. This is most evident with the recent Stand with Wet'suwet'en movement in response to the contentious Coastal GasLink pipeline project. Although blockades will remain a necessary mechanism to address immediate infringements, the future of our territories will largely be determined by whether we sustain our ties to the land and how Aboriginal title is defined at the table. We cannot neglect our territory or leave it to the Crown to define its meaning. As Wilpsters, we are the rightful heirs to our Lax'yip. A shared right and responsibility grounded in our ancestral laws, to govern our relations to the territories and to each other as we have done since the Temlaxam apocalypse.

To this end, we briefly outline a Gitxsan understanding of the sui generis nature of Aboriginal title. We call this the 'wii gyamk generous definition of Gitxsan title. It is shorthand for "big generosity under the Law of Gyamk." It represents a way out of the post-*Delgamuukw* Dark Age characterized by infighting among Houses, band councils, and our coastal neighbours over competing land claims and interests in the Lax'yip.[21] Instead of battling over resource-revenue rights premised on a faulty property model, the sovereign model of 'wii gyamk generous aims to bring back the original spirit and intent of the Lax'yip governance system as our ancestors knew it. It is, after all, only due to their hospitality that "Aboriginal title" has crystalized as a legal concept that the Crown must now reckon with. There are three features of 'wii gyamk generous title that we discern from our oral histories.

Firstly, it is a right that can only be exercised by extending big generosity to present and future generations. The Temlaxam warrior Yeel' sets the precedent here. The history recounted by 'Wii Muugulsxw states Yeel' initially wanted Anspayaxw and its surrounding territories all to himself. It was only after reflection on the futility of war and the gradual admission that he desired friendship with Ts'iiyee that they reached a sharing arrangement that served their mutual interests as well as the interests of future generations as enjoyed by their descendants in the Houses of Gitluudaahlxw and X̲hliimlax̲ha. House families remain the authoritative decision makers when it comes to their territories. Not the band council or the Crown. Socioeconomic opportunities must be decided by each House and take fully into account the impacts these decisions will have on the youngest alive today and those still to come.

Secondly, 'wii gyamk generous title rights can only be transferred to another sovereign people, and so require law enforcement powers. In her testimony, Antgulilbix shared an event that occurred "thousands of years ago" at a creek known as Xsi wis an skit. This area, Antgulilbix explains, was given "as a compensation" to her House for the killing of one of their family members named Yal who had been murdered on the ice near Xsagangaxda that runs into the Skeena River. As part of xsiisxw, the law of compensation, Antgulilbix states the offending House painted a red sun on a nearby tree, the fireweed crest representing "the compensation that's in exchange of blood and [that] won't be taken back from us until the end of the world. It will be there."[22] Building on this oral history, Gitxsan title today must provide the legal space and freedom for House families to continue to practise xsiisxw among other long-standing and new areas of law that may require territorial transfers for indeterminate or permanent periods of time.[23] This right puts into question any fixed maps of House territories and boundaries. Each House family must map and remap its Lax'yip, signing House-to-House and House-to-settler memorandums of understandings of current boundaries and any changes thereof. The recent *Cowichan Tribes v. Attorney General of Canada* decision (2025 BCSC 1490) further underscores this dynamic view of title, as the Court held that the existence of fee simple ownership does not extinguish or invalidate Aboriginal title, but rather demands new legal frameworks. In this light, Gitxsan title must be understood not as a static inheritance, but as a living legal relation, continually renewed through acts of remembrance, reciprocity, and remapping across generations as Gitxsan law necessitates.[24]

Thirdly, 'wii gyamk generous title is an inextinguishable right that ends the myths of terra nullius, the doctrine of discovery, including the myth of "underlying Crown title." In the 'wii gyamk generous paradigm, there is no such thing as justified Crown infringements. The Crown holds no unilateral power to negotiate and infringe House territories because Gitxsan title does not, contrary to the Supreme Court of Canada's 1997 decision, arise from underlying Crown title but from the ancestral generosity extended to the Temlaxam refugees over four millennia ago. It is a generosity that has been extended since contact—in the nineteenth century with the arrival of early settlers in need of food, medicine, and shelter and whose descendants remain at home on Gitxsan territories today; in the twentieth century with the migration of families from the northern villages of Kaldo'o and Kisga'ga'as into Anspayaxw where several Houses offered their own fishing sites as sources of refuge and sustenance; and in our own century with land defenders reconnecting displaced Wilpsters from the cities and reserves onto their own House territories in sustainable ways that mitigate the Gitxsan impact on climate change. In this light, today's land defence and land back efforts led by the Gitxsan and Wet'suwet'en people are a principled enactment of 'wii gyamk generous itself.

Overall, Temlaxam offers many takeaways for the times. For one, it teaches us the lasting value of careful deliberation and grassroots action to meet the needs of the people. It fell to the clans of the smaller, surrounding villages to serve as first responders to the refugee crisis. We imagine this involved extensive discussions within and between House families and clans over a significant period of time. One of the pressing concerns likely focused on how each region, populated by people we now identify as Tsimshian, Gitxsan, and Nisga'a, could safely adapt and expand its pre-existing Lax'yip governance system in ways that would avoid the Temlaxam cycles of disrespect and destruction, or at least mitigate their scale and occurrence. This remains an important consideration in relation to Canada, a capitalist state that extracts from "coast to coast to coast."[25] If Temlaxam teaches us one thing, may it be to assess our structures of governance and well-being not only in terms of capitalist accumulation but in the full light of Gyamk where the health of individuals and communities is understood to be a matter of the heart, cultivated by the Tsi'basaa ethic of sharing and caring on our territories. When our structures of governance render us indifferent to this Lax'yip ethic, when they eliminate these sensibilities from us in times of wealth and leisure, that is when we are most at risk of authoring our own ruin.

In our view, it is worth keeping this in mind as we proceed to reckon with the Crown and its corporate interests and offers. However picturesque talks of economic prosperity may sound, however much revenue may be extracted from the territories, the true test of "reconciliation" is not Crown consultation and compensation so much as it is the level of

Gyamkian compassion and principle we sustain through it all. We think here of the legendary confrontation between the Greek philosopher Diogenes and Alexander the Great.[26] The King of Macedonia had heard a lot about this old Cynic who had become famous for his wisdom and simplicity of living, so much so that the people called him Diogenes the Dog. From a Gitxsan perspective, we might call him a wolf clan relative. Content to live in a barrel in the marketplace, Diogenes awoke one morning to find Alexander standing above him. "I have power to grant you anything in my kingdom," Alexander declares. "What would you like?"

Not blinking an eye, Diogenes asked the King for just one thing: "Get out of my sunlight." Gyamkian hospitality lets us all enjoy the Sun, the simplicity of enjoying our territories without imperial intrusion. This is the nonnegotiable Lax'yip boundary worth defending across generations, on the ground, and at the table where the Crown asserts its dominion. "Get out of my sunlight." A simple expression of integrity with a power of its own to prevent a Crown recurrence of Temlaxam.

4

YUKXW/ FEAST

> Your pole records experiences of your house. It's like a history book of your house. It's evidence that [it] did exist, does exist and will continue to exist. So maintaining your poles is really important. It's a very important evidence in the Gitksan Nation, that you are what you are.
>
> —*Hanamuxw (Joan Ryan)*[1]

Yukxw (Feast) is a long-standing governance practice that continues to be organized by House families in the community halls of Anspayaxw, Sikedakhl, Gitanmaax, Kitwanga, Gitsegukla, and Gitanyow. It's how key events and decisions are legitimately acknowledged and confirmed to be true in the eyes and ears of the people under ayookxw niyee.

Historically, House families sent tee'ts, messengers, to invite guests from other Houses to attend their feasts that were either hosted on the land or in the wilp li'ligit, the cedar longhouses in which our people sat on bleachers supporting their Simgigyet, family leaders sitting in the front rows, while a big fire at the centre, a spark of Gyamk, kept them all warm.[2] There they tasted the wealth of the House's territories—its fresh waters, plants, berries, salmon, and wild game. Currency in the form of copper shields, groundhog skins, and oolichan grease, among other valuables, were offered as gifts and payments to feast witnesses. Sharing the territory in this intimate way, the yukxw marked the significant occasions of each family, from birth and child naming to death, from rites of passage for youth to marriage between Houses, from conflict and compensation to the inauguration of medicine people and chiefly successors. The yukxw is how the Gitxsan do business.

When we consider the yukxw today, we troubleshoot a few issues. Firstly, we should say the yukxw has been consistently undermined since contact by Christian churches and Canadian state officials alike. Criminalized under the Indian Act from 1884 to 1951, the feast went underground, often disguised as Christian gatherings with full-on hymn singing and opening and closing prayers. Those that were openly held were randomly shut down by the police, with family leaders being arrested on the spot. In 1921, this happened to Martha Brown's predecessor, Xhliimlaxha (Edward Sexsmith), in the middle of his House's feast. Seventy-one years old at the time, he died of pneumonia induced by a cold jail cell.[3] In addition to the Indian Act ban on the yukxw, House families experienced child abduction via the residential/day schools and Sixties Scoop and land dispossessions with the establishment of the reserve system, among other atrocities.

With these historical considerations in mind, it is understandable that the yukxw is now thoroughly Christianized and primarily focused on death feasts and headstone raisings. Although these feasts bring House families and clans together to support bereaved families and to reaffirm Gitxsan relations, we believe the yukxw can offer this support in a more spiritually inclusive, efficient, and House-empowering way through the revitalization of the bax maga gyet, pole-raising feasts. Of all the feasts in the early decades of the Indian Act potlatch ban, the bax maga gyet was the most suppressed as it was difficult for a House family to raise a fifty-foot pole under the pretense of a Christian table meeting. The ban further diminished the handing down of pole carving skills to the next generation. Many House families settled for engravings on headstones.[4]

There were, however, a handful of Houses that raised poles anyway. One comes out of the western village of Gitsegukla, from the fireweed House of Gyetm Maxmagii. In what follows, we study the precedent set by the Gyetm Maxmagii family before imagining what pole raising in the twenty-first century might look like for our House families in Anspayaxw. In so doing, we aim to show that bax maga gyet is a powerful enactment of ayookxw niyee that not only commemorates those who have passed on in the House since its last pole raising, but further raises up those still living and those still to come. Pole raising is Gyamkian in its respect and reverence for all life.

Twentieth-Century Pole-Raising Precedents

To understand the Gyetm Maxmagii family's twentieth-century pole-raising precedent, we have to go back to the nineteenth century when its Sim'oogi, Hanamuxw (Fanny Johnson), raised two poles, one of which washed away during the Skeena River flood of 1936.[5] In 1945, the succeeding Hanamuxw (Geoffrey Johnson) moved the surviving pole from Hazelton back to Gitsekgula where it was originally raised. In 1970, the pole was removed again, this time by the Gitsegukla band council without the House's consent in order to make way for a new school. Under Gitxsan law, a House's pole cannot be moved without the House's express permission. To correct the situation and reestablish its authority, the Hanamuxw family raised a new pole in 1991. The matter was the focal point of both Gwaans (Olive Ryan)'s and her daughter Hanamuxw (Joan Ryan)'s testimonies at the *Delgamuukw-Gisday'wa* trial. Based on their evidence, we identify three key features of the legal process for putting up a pole.

The first feature is the activation of the House's wilnadaahl and wilksiwitxw and the legal obligations implicit in these family relationships. It is the responsibility of the family leader to commission their father's House to take care of the pole. In the case of the pole raised in 1991, Hanamuxw (Joan Ryan) appointed her father's frog House, the Hak'w family. Wilps Hak'w then delegated the job to chief and master carver Earl Muldoe from the Delgamuukw family, a fellow frog House from Anspayaxw. At the k'ots gan ceremony in 1987, "when they cut the tree down" event, the Hanamuxw family invited several House leaders from their wilksiwitxw. The list included Lelt, Xamlaxyeltxw and Gwashl Am from Gitanyow (Geoffrey Johnson's father's House), Sinankxws, and Hak'w. As part of their duties, Lelt (Fred Johnson) and Xamlaxyeltxw (Solomon Marsden), on behalf of Gwashl Am, sang two types of songs, the xsinaahlxw and the limx oo'y. On the wilnadaahl side, Gwis Gyen (Stanley Williams) gave a speech detailing their shared fireweed histories and the territories owned by Hanamuxw. Gisday'wa (Alfred Joseph) was also present as a Wet'suwet'en witness. The Hanamuxw family provided gifts to all their kin, including xhluuhligyootxw, an axe, to the wilksiwitxw to help build the pole.[6] At the actual pole raising, the wilksiwitxw were further responsible for preparing the ground and digging the hole. With this work complete, the tim hanak, the in-laws of the House, provided the ga jaak, ropes, while all the hereditary chiefs from all the other clans and villages raised up the pole together by hand. When the 1945 pole went up, the Hanamuxw family shared three naxnox performances and songs, one dating as far back as Temlaxam. The song was also shared at the pole raising in 1991.[7]

The second feature is the legal logic and histories of the ayuks, the crests, carved into the pole. In her testimony, Gwaans details the crests on their House's 1945 pole. At the bottom is Gyetm Maxmagii, a Rainbow Being. Above this crest is a bil'ust, star, then a rainbow, followed by an upside-down man. At the top of the pole is laa'm gayt, a carving of a hat worn by Gyetm Maxmagii. These ayuks are the intellectual property of the Hanamuxw family, recounting their ancient adaawk from Temlaxam. Gwaans clarifies that there used to be a beaver crest at the bottom of the pole that eroded. She explains that the beaver crest has legal significance as it represented one of the ayuks owned by the carver's House. In this case, the carver's name was Gawa Gyanii from the frog House of Gwinuu out of Gitanyow village, a carver selected from Fanny Johnson's extended wilksiwitxw. In the case of the 1991 pole, Gwaans explains how the beaver crest will be replaced by spagim ganaa'w, a crest of six frogs owned by House of Hak'w, her daughter's immediate wilksiwitxw.[8] Gwaans teaches that ayookxw niyee requires carvers to obtain permission before using ayuks that belong to House families.[9]

The third feature pertains to the activation of the House's daxgyet, its power and legitimacy as a governing family over its territories. According to Gwaans, the main reason for raising a new pole in 1991 was to address the fact that "people were ignoring Hanamuxw"[10] during and after the Gitsegukla band council's moving of her House's pole without consent. The act not only infringed ayookxw niyee but also their daxgyet. The pole raising corrected this in a variety of ways. For one, the wilksiwitxw stepped in. Their labour, witnessing presence, and songs were done so that, as Gwaans asserts, "when the pole is raised, it will have the daxgyet of the wilksiwitxw."[11] Hanamuxw (Joan Ryan) further explains how the pole is "a way of reaffirming and confirming the Dax gyet of Hanamuxw." The pole does this by "establishing that the property of Hanamuxw has not been abandoned, nor will it be in the future." Moreover, the pole communicates to "other chiefs that the house is as strong as it was before, and that it will continue to exist because we do have a fair number of people . . . who will continue with the activities within the House of Hanamuxw who will ensure that it will continue in the future."[12]

Taken together, the pole activates the legal obligations in a House's wilnadaahl and wilksiwitxw, captures the legal logic and histories of the House, and affirms the House's continued authority to uphold its legal order on its territories. In this way, the House uses the occasion to commemorate all of those who have died since the House's last pole raising. Hanamuxw (Don Ryan) speaks about this part of the proceeding:

> It's also a way of releasing the spirits of those who have passed on. It's a way of giving thanks for having had them in your house. It's a way of giving recognition to the contributions that they have made to your house. It's a way of acknowledging to our creator too the privilege of having had them share their lives with you. It's a way of saying that we have completed the business of caring for them. It's a way of saying that they have added a dimension to our lives. And when I say our lives I'm talking about the members of my house, and to you as an individual. And it's a way of saying that we respect them, and we are saying that they were important to us.[13]

Gwaans too speaks of the occasion known as dim am bax yees. What is significant to note in her testimony is that all the deceased, even those who held the highest chief names, were remembered by their baby names. Here she orates a part of the remembrance:

> They mention—they use the baby name. They didn't call the chief name. They use the baby name when they do that. They call them, you know, the ones that deceased. That's the reason why the pole was up, after the pole was up, and that's what they do at the Feasting. When they holding the blanket like this and they called the baby name: Dim am bax yees, Baasx, Dim am bax yees Asi bax, Dim am bax yees, amx tsii kaa'y, Dim am bax yees wildim waax. Baby names. That's what they did, and the chiefs, they're witnesses.[14]

As a further commemoration, the baby names of all the deceased are engraved on the House's pole.[15] So there is a substantive process built into the bax maga gyet equivalent to today's Christian death and headstone raising feasts. As the current Hanamuxw (Don Ryan) has taught us, our ancestors practised cremation as it was believed this allowed the oots'in, the human spirit, to reincarnate back into the House family as soon as possible. While death feasts did occur, they were reserved for those who held the most prominent chiefly names in a House. All Wilpsters who passed on were cremated and later honoured at their family's pole raising. Thus, carved poles are memory poles. They make known the House's family relationships, histories, territorial title rights, and the legacies of all their loved ones who passed on. They are made with the hope of reincarnating it all again with each new pole and each new life raised by the House.

Pole Raising in the Twenty-First Century

Inspired by the precedent set by the Hanamuxw family, here we exercise our legal imagination by pondering what pole raising might look like for the Git'tsim'gedimgyat family today. Git'tsim'gedimgyat is a practical case in point for a few reasons. First, as the House leader Sim'oogit Hawaaw (Marilyn Wright)'s fireweed father is Tsi'basaa (Stanley Wilson), the Git'tsim'gedimgyat family would commission the fireweed House of Git'luuhl'um'hetxwit as the wilksiwitxw responsible for the pole. Both of our House families would therefore be partners in a Git'tsim'gedimgyat pole raising. The second reason to focus on Git'tsim'gedimgyat is that it was represented by X̱hliimlax̱ha (Martha Brown) during the *Delgamuukw-Gisday'wa* trial. This left Git'tsim'gedimgyat unrecognized in official maps created during the litigation and neglected in later political negotiations and corporate projects affecting its territories. Git'tsim'gedimgyat has thus been overlooked as a governing House family with its own history, names, crests, and territories. A pole raising would correct this oversight and affirm all of these distinctions. It would be a reaffirmation and confirmation of Git'tsim'gedimgyat's daxgyet. The third reason to consider Git'tsim'gedimgyat is that the House has not raised a pole in over 100 years. The pole of the Tall-hat was raised in the mid-1860s and the Garment-of-the-Eagle pole was raised in the 1880s, likely just before the potlatch ban.[16] Over this time, the poles eroded and are no longer standing in the village. This is likely the situation facing many House families today. Our investigating, troubleshooting, and envisioning here is thus offered to support the collaborative efforts needed to revitalize pole raising across Houses. In this regard, we consider three common components: the feast process, family collaboration, and the innovation of ayuks that reflect ancient and recent histories.

For a sense of the process, we consulted the current Hanamuxw (Don Ryan), who teaches us that pole raising consists of a cycle of five feasts. The first is a small planning feast wherein the House announces its intentions to put up a pole. The second feast is the lagam'yatsa, or woodchip feast, in which the House details who has been commissioned to carve the pole and acknowledges the role of the wilksiwitxw in the proceedings. In the third feast, the pole is complete and is welcomed by the people. As part of the procession, it is customary that the children of the House ride on the pole as it is driven into the village. In the fourth feast, the pole is raised, and all the people who have passed on since the last pole are fully acknowledged and remembered. A year later, a fifth and final feast is held, known as the gwalgwa, to "dry off" the pole. This is the occasion for the House to recite all of its properties: its songs, names, histories, crests, territorial holdings, and dramatic naxnox performances. The whole cycle varies in time, anywhere from two years or longer. The pole raised by Hanamuxw (Joan Ryan) in 1991 cost about $50,000 ($1,000 per linear foot), with a total feast expense of $120,000. Hanamuxw (Don Ryan) tells us that, on principle, his Wilp generated these funds from their own resources without the assistance of grants.

This brings us to consider the extensive level of family collaboration required to put up a feast today. The House planning would first involve an agreed-upon financial budget, including contributions from each Wilpster. As it is the House leader's responsibility, they would contribute the most, followed by wing-chiefs and Wilpsters. Initial timeframes for both fundraising and the feasts would be another planning necessity. To determine this, the Git'tsim'gedimgyat family would need to consult with Git'luuhl'um'hetxwit about the estimated cost and time needed for their carver to complete the pole. Here it is important to note that due to a shortage of Gitxsan master carvers generally, Git'luuhl'um'hetxwit might need to delegate the commissioned work to a carver outside of their House. This may require additional time. There would also have to be planning around the tools and gifts for each of the five feasts (including the purchase of the ropes by the in-laws), invitations to House families in the village, and the ongoing contact with the wilksiwitxw about their feast involvement and updates on the pole. Git'tsim'gedimgyat's wilnadaahl—X̲hliimlax̲ha and Malii—would also need to be consulted and involved to speak about their shared history with Git'tsim'gedimgyat and confirm its crests, names, and territories, just as Gwis Gyen (Stanley Williams) did for the Hanamuxw family.

This takes us to the matter of ayuks and the legal histories that would need to be carved into a new Git'tsim'gedimgyat pole. There are some examples of House families raising a pole with the same crest designs over three generations, with only the father's House's crest at the bottom changing.[17] That said, we believe the situation we face today calls for innovations in ayuks that fully reflect the past two centuries of enduring genocide as House families. This recent history now forms part of each House's adaawk in addition to its ancient past, what Hanamuxw (Don Ryan) calls the sii adaawk.

With this in mind, at the bottom of the new Git'tsim'gedimgyat pole would be a crest owned by Git'luuhl'um'hetxwit. If the pole was delegated out, the carver's House crest would also be featured. Next there would be a combination of ancient crests from the Tall-hat and Garment-of-the-Eagle poles. The former pole contains only one crest of a person sitting down, wearing a high conical hat on their head. It was adopted after a Git'tsim'gedimgyat family member was killed by a Nisg̲a'a man believed to be from a wolf House in Gitwinksilk. The crest is a xsiisxw, or compensation, for the murder. The latter pole featured an eagle named Small Eagle used to top the pole. Five human beings hung from its claws, one grasping the legs of the other above in a chain. These crests record the travails of Kwarxkik, the House's founding ancestor. In the adaawk, he loses all of his House's property to lahal, bone games. Later, he recovers it all back with the naxnox aid of huu'umst, the power of devil's club medicine, and the help of an eagle clan family.[18] Throughout his struggles he earns many new crests, including the name Gwaxskiik. Below the crests documenting this history, there is the top half of a bear protruding out of the pole near the bottom. This crest details Hawaaw's ancient relationship with the wolf House of Malii in Gitanyow. It recounts a time when a matriarch in their House went missing. They eventually found her in a canoe with a grizzly. The warriors in the Malii-Hawaaw family rescued her and killed the bear. When Hawaaw branched off over an irresolvable matrimonial dispute, they parted with the top half of the bear crest while Malii kept the hindquarters.[19] Finally, new ayuks may be created by Git'tsim'gedimgyat artists to commemorate the House overcoming the last two centuries of shared adversities like the residential and day schools, the Sixties and Millennial scoops, Indian Act land dispossession, the *Delgamuukw* litigation, and ongoing settler infringements on Hawaaw's territories.

Taking this brief overview into account, suffice it to say that the feast process, family collaboration, and crest making required to put up a new Hawaaw pole is a major undertaking. It requires a profound level of belief, patience, and diplomacy throughout the course, especially on the part of the family leaders. It not only requires hawal, financial contributions, from all in the House, but just as much requires the House to do the relational work of building strong wilksiwitxw ties with Git'luuhl'um'hetxwit. It requires drawing on the gifts and talents of everyone in the Git'tsim'gedimgyat family, from the artists to the land defenders, in order to do such a daring thing as to raise up a pole after a century-plus hiatus.

And so it is helpful to picture the fruits of the labour. The Git'tsim'gedimgyat children giggling and cheering as they ride the pole into Anspayaxw. The Git'tsim'gedimgyat grannies and grandpas, the mommies and daddies, the aunties and uncles, all glowing with pride. The Git'luuhl'um'hetxwit family standing there strong in front, backing Git'tsim'gedimgyat just as they have over a multigenerational wedded alliance. Imagine as well the many hands on the pole, pushing it upwards, the daxgyet and power channelling through, the songs heard moving in the winds, with all the eyes on this little House refusing to be crushed by settler-colonial genocide. Finally, picture this: Kwarxkik and the ancestors and all those who have passed on since the late nineteenth century revelling in this historic moment, this reincarnation of an entire lawful people, and this thing of governance called the yukxw. It all brings to mind what the Jewish philosopher Spinoza stated so long ago, "All things excellent are as difficult as they are rare."[20] Pole raising is that rare and excellent thing that requires the difficult work of law. Pole raising is Gitxsan law in action, showing the world that we *still* are what we are.

Our short study of pole raising in the twentieth and twenty-first centuries is offered to inaugurate a far more expansive field of yukxw studies and practices, a branch within a growing wilpography. By focusing on the pole-raising feast, our main point has been to demonstrate that the life and times of our House families are about so much more than funerals and headstones. Twenty-first-century feasts should celebrate the birth and naming of our children, mark their safe passages into adulthood, recognize and enjoy the first spring salmon they catch, the first mountain goat they hunt, the first devil's club medicine they harvest and make into a necklace; honour their graduations; confer upon them names befitting their talents and contributions; and witness their sacred marriage vows, among other amazing moments worth observing as a lawful people, as we have always done. This celebratory feasting may also bring us back to hosting yukxw on our own territories, making soups and foods from the plants, fish, animals, and berries harvested there, and rebuilding those cedar longhouses known as the wilp li'ligit. An architectural design that may help us be solid like a sgano once more.

With all this enterprise, we may even raise up feasting itself across generations in a global age of spiritual diversity where our commitment to freedom of belief is a model for all democratic constitutions and legal orders worth their soup and salt.[21] The key ingredients for this are the same as those found active in a Wilpster Uprising: a spicy hagwil jam blend of Wilp, Pdeek, Lax'yip, g̲ant Yukxw—the House, the clan, the territory, and the feast. With these we have the bare bones of Gitxsan legal culture and the possibility of making a new day.

PART 2

GYAMKIAN FORMATIONS

5

SISATXW/ MAKING A NEW DAY

> The way we used to take care of ourselves, the medicines we used to keep. And the ceremonies that we used to do, that has fallen by the wayside in our march toward gaining legal rights in this country. I think we need to rebuild that spirit, because it is that spirit that connects you to your land. You need to go and sit, bare-ass if you have to, and sit on the land and talk to your grandmothers, and we have to do that.
>
> *—Dimdiigibuu, Ardythe Wilson, cited in Napoleon, "Ayook," 239*

The fireweed matriarch Dimdiigibuu (Ardythe Wilson) calls us to wake up to sisatxw, a Gitxsanimx̱ term that translates as "making a new day." Sisatxw is an ancestral discipline that involves one's entire lifestyle, from diet to exercise to daily decisions about conduct and relationships. It occurs before every significant life event facing Wilpsters and their House families, from birth to puberty to the adult labours of growing wise and taking care of one's family. One of the recurring themes in recorded oral histories is how Gitxsan people forget to practise ayookxw niyee and experience hardship. Yet in each dilemma faced there are always a few Wilpsters who meet the moment and shape Gitxsan history for the better. In fact, it is often the youth who are said to have pursued solitude on their territories.[1] After a period of reflection, these Wilpsters find guidance from the sbil naxnox, the spirits of the land,

and the insight to make decisions that ultimately avert or safely respond to a given disaster. This liberating sojourn is sisatxw.

As we think about our present moment in history, we believe genocide and settler-colonial realities can be overcome with the full reincarnation of sisatxw. In this regard, precedent has been set in the area of addiction recovery, most notably the Wilp Si'satxw/House of Purification Treatment Centre located in Kitwanga, British Columbia. Sisatxw can similarly contribute solutions to other pressing issues, including mental health, crime and incarceration, education, and the rebuilding of our legal orders. Indeed, sisatxw has been an integral part of our collaborative work on *The Gyamkian Revolution*. We hold ourselves and each other accountable to what we write and share with the world. We speak honestly about our struggles and draw strength from the insights generated by our bond. We have found that sisatxw helps if only in providing the necessary space from the toxic colonial-capitalist cultures, structures, and systems that cause, normalize, and escalate many of the world's problems. To guide fresh-air breakthroughs and solutions that can benefit us all, we look at oral histories that detail the essential features of sisatxw, from bathing and fasting to harvesting and consuming bush medicine. We highlight the Gitxsan vision logic behind these disciplines and how Gyamk once again provides the cosmic clarity and coherence to this continual rite of passage into lawful living.

The Revolution Begins with Bathing and Fasting

From a Gitxsan perspective, bathing in open waters is about rejuvenating our ancestral connection to Gyamk. After 'Nii Ts'iits Ska'wo approves her granddaughter Ska'wo's marriage to Gyetm Maxmagii, the couple leave the devastated Keemelay village and travel to an alternate universe where Gyamk, the cosmic source of Gyetm Maxmagii, resides. It is in this universe that Ska'wo gave birth to her first baby through the power of light rays. Upon the birth of his first grandchild, it is said Gyamk "beamed as never before in the sky."[2] It was a celebration not only of new life but of the "open ways of life" having overcome "all obstacles that swarm everywhere under cover" on Earth.[3] Gyamk formed a close bond with his grandchild, Ligii yuun. "He would hold him every morn in his arms, gaze complacently into his face, bathe him in the milky fountain of Maudeks at dawn, and stretch his limbs one by one, thus inducing rapid growth; until, at the *kuhlarrantu*—the half moon—the child stood on his feet and walked for the first time around his father's lodge."[4] In this way, Gyamk welcomed all of Ska'wo's children, holding each in his arms, bathing them and stretching their limbs four times each day, envisioning the beauty of each grandchild's "sun-lit maturity."[5]

When the children reached puberty they turned to Grandpa Gyamk for guidance. "And the Sun ancestor lavished upon his human family the gifts and powers that would soon restore Keemelay to its former seat on the banks of the Skeena."[6] Gyamk imparted to each "a clear insight" into all areas of Gitxsan lawful life, from the nature of all species to the rigours of fishing, canoe making, building houses, and providing food and refuge to their families wherever they might venture during the four earthly seasons.[7] The capstone of this grandfatherly training was the Law of Gyamk expressed in four principles: respect all species and their young; commit to fasting before all important events across the lifespan; show regard for the deceased by mourning them and cremating their remains; and, last but not least, continue in awe of the Gyamkian cosmos itself. For life on Earth is Gyamk's seed and "growth his daily concern."[8] With these rules regulating their hearts, the Gyamkian grandkids land on the muddy banks of the Skeena River to rebuild the Keemelay village and eventually a home in the ancient city of Temlaxam.

This account provides the cosmic context for understanding the significance of bathing and fasting in later oral histories. For instance, when a famine strikes Temlaxam after the snowfall ruined the city (as recounted by Antgulilbix in Chapter 3), it was the eldest nephew of Neas Hiwas who took up the call of sisatxw. The nephew began by sitting quietly and listening to the older generation discuss solutions to the problem. "It was only proper and expedient that the youth should become familiar with what lay ahead," writes Neas-D-Hok, as only then could "he be prepared to take up his task when the time came."[9] Having listened to all the points and perspectives, Neas Hiwas's nephew initiated his "rites of purification" in the dry month known as lasimedeek. These rites involved fasting and self-sacrifice. In the corner of his House, he "washed himself" for three days. On the fourth day, he moved to the next corner, and again he washed. Two other days were spent in this corner without washing. He followed this sequence in the third and fourth corners as well. Twelve days pass in all: fasting, drinking sparingly, and chewing the inner bark of the devil's club. The plant medicine "purged him and brought out impurities through the pores in beads of sweat."[10] These twelve days did not complete the task, however. He persevered, moving to another House and repeating the whole sequence yet again. This continued through many seasons, "until the warming rays of Gyamk once more began to lower the deep snow levels."[11] In the springtime, the young man completed his task. Fifteen Houses had been purified, and he attained his own naxnox, spirit power. His work strengthened him as he set forth to find new hunting grounds for his people, a land known today as Neas-D-Hok's fireweed territories near the village of Kitselas.[12] Sisatxw is the youth-initiated response to environmental upheaval that sparked the safe journey of the first Temlaxam refugees.

In this spirit, sisatxw is a practice that connects coastal peoples in peaceful alliances. We see this occurring in the recorded Hawaaw oral histories. After losing all of his House property and family members in the ancient game of lahal, bone games, it is said Kwarxkik, the eldest nephew, became suicidal. In desperation, he fled his village until he found a creek surrounded by devil's club. "For many days he ate nothing but the stalks of this plant, and he became very thin; his flesh was all gone. He lived there for many years, often bathing in the creek nearby."[13] The sbil naxnox, the spirits of the place, eventually respond to help Kwarxkik. The scales of a salmon transform into copper shields, the currency of the time, while the supernatural woman of the devil's club marries him and teaches him new gambling strategies to regain his House family and property. With this aid, he returns to his village and wins everything back and then some, only to lose it all again to his resentful rivals, who send him down the river in a gummed-up canoe. Facing his demise, Kwarxkik is rescued by an eagle clan family.[14] They adopt him and teach him new skills as a sea hunter. Much of his training is the work of sisatxw, of "sitting by himself" and watching his adopted family "very closely."[15] This is how "they instructed him" and how he learned to transform into an eagle like them. "Early in the morning," it is said he would successfully hunt whales, seals, and sea lions. Witnessing his labours, the sbil naxnox of the ocean soon responded. One day, a pole was seen sticking out of the saltwater in front of the village. It was only thanks to Kwarxkik's "great strength" that his adopted House was able to bring it to shore.[16] As his daxgyet, his power as a Wilpster, had been restored, his adopted House gave him new crests and a new name, Gwaxskiik, before encouraging him to return home.[17] These distinct eagle crests were later recorded on one of the Hawaaw poles, an ancestral reminder that sisatxw can be practised anywhere and with anyone, even with eagles flying over the sea.

In more recent history, Sim'oogit Gwis Gyen (Stanley Williams), from the fireweed House of Gitsegukla, gave commissioned evidence for *Delgamuukw-Gisday'wa* that details his knowledge and practice of sisatxw. As sisatxw is kept private among Houses, Gwis Gyen is careful in what he shares:

> I'll tell you just a short one. If a young person, a single person, when he goes through this sisatxw, what he does is he bath[e]s for four days. As he finishes—each time he finishes taking a bath, they . . . make a ring of the devil's club, and he would go through this each time he takes a bath . . . and each time he would do this, four days, then he would go to bed but he would sleep the other way: where his head was his feet will be. And each time . . . he would eat the plant of the devil's club, he would eat about three inch[es] of this. That's under the bark of the devil's club.[18]

This observance goes on for about a month. In this time, Gwis Gyen emphasizes that the "person that is going through this sisatxw has to be always busy and what he does is he usually goes on his territories just to keep busy. And if he doesn't do that, then the sisatxw won't turn out the way he wants it to be."[19] Gwis Gyen's knowledge of sisatxw was taught to him by his father Ts'iiyee (George Williams) from the House of 'Wii Muugulsxw. When he was seventeen, Gwis Gyen remembers how his father practised sisatxw:

> In the evening when he was training me how to travel on the mountain to get the goats, what my father did is he cut off the hooves of the goat and he put it on the fire . . . until the hooves came off . . . the bone, and he took the hooves and he put it on my toes . . . while he was doing this, the hooves are still hot and . . . after this he takes the hooves and . . . goes up to the mountain and he puts these hooves in the cracks of the mountain. After . . . he came down and he takes a bath four times . . . in the water . . . after I went to the mountain I

> could feel that, what my father did by the purification. I could feel it when I was travelling up to the mountains. Whenever I . . . chase a goat on the mountain, it's just like a flat surface for me. It doesn't seem rough at all.[20]

As an adult, Gwis Gyen enjoyed great success as a mountain goat hunter in his own right. During one expedition he shot forty-two in one day. Of his mountain climbing he said it was so effortless it was like "running through a field."[21]

From Neas Hiwas's nephew to Kwarxkik to Gwis Gyen and his father Ts'iiyee, what all of these historical accounts teach us is that sisatxw is the enduring constant in the life and times of all lawful peoples under the Sun. Whether washing in the four corners of a House, or bathing in a creek, or in an ocean, or while throwing hooves on the mountainside, these enactments of sisatxw all along the northwest coast and across generations are full circular turns back to that cosmic caretaking our ancestors once experienced in a milky creek called Maudeks. The water wherein Ska'wo's babes were held and bathed in the warm light of Gyamk. The water wherein each of their four limbs experienced exponential growth so that they might one day walk gently on Earth according to the Law of Gyamk. It remains so today, if only we rebuild that spirit of sisatxw as Dimdiigibuu encourages us to do. Whatever the obstacles that swarm our times, we need to remember that the open ways of life that can help remedy the situation, those buzzing ways of being that constitute the Gyamkian Revolution, humbly begin with bathing and fasting in algorithms of four. When we call up Gyamk in this way, a naxnox sooner or later answers and lets us know the cosmos has our back.

The Revolution Is Fuelled by Bush Medicine

Sisatxw is undertaken at various degrees of intensity. Fasting and bathing on the territory for a set number of days falls on the strong end of the spectrum. Daily reminders offered by relatives to "use your ears" or "walk gently" fall on the lighter end. At whatever intensity, what we see from the oral histories cited above is that bush medicine energizes this revolutionary practice. During her testimony, Gwaans (Olive Ryan) spoke of many medicines on her territory: devil's club, water lily roots, wild celery, maalgwasxw, high bush cranberries mixed with oolichan grease, the inner bark of the balsam tree, and the pitch of spruce tree and jack pine. She shared her medicine knowledge for one sole purpose: "to help the people" as her grandmother did and taught her to do.[22] The most prominent medicine in this regard is devil's club, or better said in Gitxsanimx̲, huu'umst or wuu'ms.[23]

In his ethnographic records, Marius Barbeau noted the medicine for its potent ability to produce "fortitude and exaltation" among the Gitxsan people.[24] Indeed, it features in numerous other coastal histories as the active ingredient that helps restore the downtrodden—broke gamblers, starving hunters, and grieving families—back to health and to good standing.[25] Here we want to spend some time learning more about this thorny plant, a fierce shrub that has flowered on the territories for over 10,000 years. For fireweed family guidance, we draw on the testimonies of Gitluudaahlxw (Pete Muldoe) and Antgulilbix (Mary Johnson), who detail how to gather the medicine and how it saved the life of a Hawaaw Wilpster named John Brown in the early twentieth century.

Gitluudaahlxw suggests the best time to harvest huu'umst is "before the leaves have started or late in the fall."[26] There are special places where it grows on the territories, and he advises to go "further back to get a bigger" stalk, which is easier to work with. Then comes the peeling of the bark. First the outer bark and then the inner parts. At this point, the medicine can be boiled into a liquid with spruce, balsam, mountain ash, and mountain juniper to make the famous Gitxsan 5-Alive blend of Indian tea. Alternatively, the inner bark can be scraped and kept in a container or a bag and left to hang dry for a few days. Afterwards, it can be crushed into a powder. In this form, Gitluudaahlxw and his partner took the medicine on a daily basis.[27] He started taking it when he wasn't feeling well a decade or so before the trial. Based on his experience, he affirmed that "it will cure you from your arthritis or anything rheumatic, anything like that."[28]

Antgulilbix gives us further insight into its curative powers. When Brown was still a youth he became sick while staying in the village of Kisg̲a'g̲a'as. "He was dying they said, he is got nothing but skin and bone. And they called this disease X'yansxw."[29] In English, this illness is known as tuberculosis. Antgulilbix then explains how the people at Kisg̲a'g̲a'as treated him with huu'umst, rolling it into little balls "like the size of the large pea," and he "chewed those things and swallow[ed] them."[30] Afterwards, Brown "got better and he got his strength back again." In her signature style of testimony, Antgulilbix shares a humorous anecdote to dramatize Brown's restored health:

> And in later years after he is an elder man, he works for the coast, he is a contractor of some boats, and a government boat happens to come around to X-ray the Indians. And people are still in the suits or clothes when they stand to have an X-ray, and there was one of his lungs is half gone they said, and they were really amazed to see what happened. This was long before the white people find out a cure for T.B. If they got T.B. they would die right there, but not among the Indians.[31]

It is worth noting that after Antgulilbix shared this story in the courtroom, Justice Allan McEachern interjected to ask Peter Grant, legal counsel for the Gitxsan-Wet'suwet'en, about the relevance of bush medicine. "Mr. Grant, how is this going to help the resolution of this case? There may be a great many of these herbal remedies that are common all over the world. How is it going to help us to resolve this case?"[32] In response, Grant stated that part of the defence was the people's use of the resources on the territories.

Be that as it may, this exchange really brings home Dimdiigibuu's point about how our efforts to gain legal rights in this country have come at the expense of neglecting "the way we used to take care of ourselves." In the tin ears of Justice McEachern, stories about how we take care of ourselves come as an "anecdotal intrusion"—an inadmissible hearsay that is "not the slightest bit helpful."[33] This gives us much pause to reflect and to say that as much as the *Delgamuukw-Gisday'wa* court action forced the Crown to finally acknowledge that Aboriginal title rights have not been extinguished and that our oral histories evidence our ownership and jurisdiction over our territories, Justice McEachern's remarks should push us to think about where revolution can really occur. In our view, it will not be in the courthouse but rather in those open ways of life nourished in our spirits and lived out among our families, harvesting our medicines on our territories and serving them up in large, pea-size portions to anyone in need of fortitude and exaltation. Bush medicine is the food and fuel of true revolution. The coup d'état stories of its continued use are an *antidotal* intrusion to the toxic cultures common to colonial-capitalist states all over the world.

For thousands of years, sisatxw has generated, time and again, an accumulation of insights that bring about entirely new ways of seeing a situation and so to leading a better life. Genocides, natural disasters, dangerous migrations, gambles gone wrong, sicknesses to the brink of death, among many other dire predicaments, have been faced by Wilpsters and their House families. Those who survived did so through sisatxw. Yet sisatxw ain't easy. It demands nothing less than the recalibration of our legal consciousness and agency in the messy midst of unfortunate circumstances. It is hard work but it is work worth doing, bare-ass if need be. For it is the only dignified way of restoring our individual and collective daxgyet. Our staying power, our 'wii bil'ust, consists in this cosmic caretaking of ours.

Contrary to Albert Camus's *The Myth of Sisyphus*, we might say that sisatxw carries anti-Sisyphean sensibilities, renouncing as it does the view that we face an absurd situation of toiling unto death in an indifferent universe.[34] For with tragic optimism, sisatxw takes life to be meaningful when we distill just a pea-size amount of refining power from our pain.[35] Sisatxw teaches that it is only in its distilled form—purified suffering, the form called healing—that we find the muscle to make a new day possible. Sisatxw helps us to ultimately see that this universe is bubbling and bathing in sbil naxnox, spirit power protection, spilling over and splashing all around with a smiling Mr. Sunshine.[36]

6

'WII BIL'UST/ STAR POWER

I'm so proud of you, baby boy. I love you so much. You're so smart! You're doing such a good job!

—Gulas Walp (Gordon Johnson) wilps Tsi'basaa

The Gyamkian Revolution is about launching the youth into the world in the same spirit as Gulas Walp (Gordon Johnson), a Gitxsan man remembered for showering those he knew with grandfatherly praise and affirmation. This is what he did when one of us, Kolin, would be within a metre-and-a-half proximity to him in the Feast Hall. Gulas Walp's words remain a treasured encouragement for Kolin as they often came after long semester sojourns away from home. Gulas Walp holds 'wii bil'ust, the star power we exercise when we give ourselves and others the warmth, care, and trust that enlivens our innate worth and goodness. Making a new day is about permeating our legal culture with this kind of wilp love that contributes to the growth and well-being of all, from the youngest to the oldest. It is this kind of legal culture we want our children, grandkids, nephews, nieces, and little cousins to inherit. We want the next generation to have the life skills, tools, and supports that will see them glow up as lawful Gitxsan stars. A true Wilpster Uprising is harnessed by our star power, and so, building on Gulas Walp's legacy, our aim in this chapter is to map out new ways we may continue to harness our star power today.

We believe this involves ensuring our ancestral cosmology remains compatible with the worldviews we may hold at any given point in our lives. We thus bring Gyamk into dialogue with Albert Einstein's democratic notion of cosmic religion, detailing how a range of religions, spiritualties, pop cultures, and the sciences may enrich the way we see the Gyamkian cosmos and live out Gitxsan law in the twenty-first century and beyond. We then go on to consider some of the global thought leaders in the field of trauma, social work, and medicine who lecture and podcast about the necessity of building meaningful connections and emotional intelligence within communities as a protection against the invasively toxic cultures of colonial-capitalist states. We engage the insights of the American psychologist Janina Fisher, social work researcher Brené Brown, and the Canadian medical doctor and trauma specialist Gabor Maté to formulate an equation that balances taking care of ourselves with taking care of each other amid the real-world realities we face. We call this way of relating the fission and fusion of Gyamk.

Gyamk in the Relative Light of Einstein

Most of our accounts of Gyamk go back to the early twentieth-century ethnographic archive. Neas-D-Hok (Walter Wright), Gusg̲ai'in (William Beynon), and Marius Barbeau represent Gyamk as a grandfather Sun figure who sustains justice through his naxnox, the spirits of the land.[1] In the Temlaxam adaawk, for instance, it is the spirits of the trout, the mountain goat, and the sky that uphold law and order. While these accounts are essential sources for learning about the Gyamkian cosmos, it is the work of our generation and the next to interpret our oral histories in ways that are grounded in compassion and wonderment for the world we live in today.

In this respect, Einstein is a Gyamkian ally and a contemporary of Neas-D-Hok, Gusg̲ai'in, and Barbeau. In *Cosmic Religion*, published in 1931, Einstein breaks out of religious literalism and defends research and science as a higher form of reverence for life and the universe. To this end, he outlines three kinds of experiences that historically gave rise to religious thought and practice. The first is the experience of fear. Homo sapiens, as a means of managing their many fears—of hunger, wild animals, sickness, and death—imagined a God-like being whom they could revere and draw on for protection. Einstein suggests this religion of fear is stabilized by a priestly class that mediates between the deity and the people. In turn, to secure their power political leaders built alliances with these spiritual leaders. The second is the experience of social feelings. While parents care for their children and leaders guide their citizens, when they come to face their own fallible and mortal natures, they long to receive the same care and guidance they offer to the vulnerable. This yearning gives rise to a moral conception of God, one that does more than reward and punish. This higher power "loves and provides for the life of the race, or of mankind, or who even loves life itself."[2] These two kinds of religion often overlap or evolve out of each other, as Einstein discerns happening in Judaism.

The third kind of religious sense comes out of the experience of feeling "the vanity of human desires and aims, and the nobility and marvelous order which are revealed in nature and in the world of thought."[3] This cosmic sense is not limited by church and dogma. It arises among heathens, heretics, and holy saints alike. It is a sensibility shared by the Greek "laughing" philosopher Democritus (circa 460–370 BC), known for developing the atomic theory of the universe and living by an ethic of cheerfulness; the Italian mystic Francis of Assisi (1182–1226), the patron saint of ecology; and the Jewish philosopher Benedict de Spinoza (1632–1677), the first modern theorist of democracy.[4] As this sense does not lead to a definite conception of God or to an official theology, Einstein calls on artists and scientists of his time to help "arouse and keep alive this feeling in those who are receptive."[5] Indeed, he maintains it is the scientific law of causality, the law of inner and outer necessity, which makes fear-based and moral religions redundant. On this point, Einstein clarifies that science does not lead to moral relativity. Rather, he affirms the "ethical behavior of man is best based on sympathy, education, and social relationships, and requires no support from religion. Man's plight would, indeed, be sad if he had to be kept in order through fear of punishment and hope of rewards after death."[6] Moreover, it is the cosmic religious sense that has empowered the great scientific discoveries, from Kepler to Newton to all earnest people of research who carry on their lonely work in long years, amid skeptics and critics to boot, just to understand and share "even a small glimpse of the reason revealed in the world."[7] The cosmic religious sense nourishes and grows all of humanity's greatest innovations. It is a Gyamkian sensibility at heart, an unwavering commitment to new life.

In bringing Gyamk into the relative light of Einstein, it is important to clarify a couple of things. Firstly, we do not subscribe to the primitive/civilized binary and its attendant belief in Western progress implicit in the three kinds of religious experience. Einstein himself troubleshoots the limits of his model, admitting that so-called religions of fear cannot be ascribed to "primitive" societies while moral religions are deemed to be the features of "civilized" ones. To illustrate this point, he invokes the Psalms of David, a book of the Old Testament, as a genuine expression of the cosmic awe he speaks of. Einstein seems to say here, and we agree, that religious sensibility does not follow a linear progression but is rather a dynamic orientation shaped by both external pressures (from spiritual leaders to political structures of governance) and internal concerns (from crises to celebratory occasions). As with any worldview, a Gyamkian outlook negotiates and is inflected by these perennial features of human life. There is always the potential that our sense of Gyamk can be secured in a definite cast (the ethnographic archive, say) or be freshly conceived in ways that resonate with new realities. The cross-pressure created between these two possibilities calls us to be compassionate towards our shared fallibility found in our own and others' conceptual limitations and ambitions.

Secondly, while we agree with Einstein that lawful living does not require religion, we believe religious and spiritual traditions can help widen the Gyamkian circle of compassion. In this regard, the Tsimshian law scholar Patricia Vickers has brought into her discussion of ancestral laws such revolutionaries as Mahatma Ghandi from the Hindu tradition, Martin Luther King Jr. from the Protestant tradition, Mother Theresa from the Catholic tradition, and Thich Nhat Hanh from the Zen Buddhist tradition, to help her people choose "pathways of love."[8] We remain open to how such perspectives may enrich and expand Gitxsan cosmology. Take, for instance, how Thich Nhat Hanh reflects upon the Sun: "We know that if our heart stops beating, the flow of our life will stop, and so we cherish our heart very much. Yet we do not often take the time to notice that other things, outside of bodies, are also essential for our survival. Look at the immense light we call the sun. If it were to stop shining, the flow of our life would also stop, so the sun is our second heart, a heart outside of our body."[9] From Zen Buddhism to the Batman beacon of pop culture to the sciences, there are many understandings that may enhance and nourish our sense of reverence for the Gyamkian cosmos.

Consider, for example, the material existence of the Sun itself. What we learn from earnest researchers is that it emerged some 4.6 billion years ago out of the recycled elements that exploded into interstellar space from the first stars of the universe some 14 billion years ago. Although assessed to be average compared with the 400 billion other stars in the Milky Way Galaxy, as the closest second-generation star to Earth, the Sun's gravitational pull holds us and all the other planets in our solar system together. Its light and heat affect all of the objects in the solar system, and we would have no life on Earth without its energy. In fact, in just one second the Sun emits more energy than humans have in 10,000 years. This energy warms our days, lights our world, and fuels the plants that give oxygen to the animals so that they may freely breathe and live and have their beings. All flora and fauna rely on the Sun's presence and power for growth.[10] That said, scientists estimate the Sun's core will run out of hydrogen in 7 billion years. It has a definite beginning and an end. In our view, this means the Sun is not something to deify but to appreciate as a symbol of the cyclical nature of life and growth itself. Gyamk does not die with the Sun but lives on in the spaces of life to be.

To know the Sun in these ways adds depth to how we relate to Gyamk as a grandfather, a ye'e. Of the Gitxsan oral tradition, it is said the stories live on the "breath of our grandfathers."[11] So significant is the term it is paired with the Gitxsanimx̱ word for law—ayookxw niyee—the laws of our breathing ancestors. We need our ancestral laws to live and grow under the Sun. Gyamk is that reincarnational element that survives first-generation stellar explosions and first-world genocides alike.

Caring for Ourselves + Each Other = The Fission and Fusion of Gyamk

The presence of Gyamk, then, is found in nourishing the spaces of life within ourselves and in our relationships with those who orbit our lives. In the Gitxsan governance system, Hanamuxw (Don Ryan) speaks of the "fission and fusion" of House families, splitting off from other Houses and joining others as integrated kin throughout history in order to care for the needs of all Wilpsters. Sometimes this means respecting a House's space. To harken back to Diogenes, there are times when we simply need to step out of other people's light. In this respect, Hanamuxw (Don Ryan) translates Gyamk as the warmth and power generated by all the stars in their manifold constellations.[12] Within these constellations, we envision our individual and collective star power as the 'wii bil'ust, the bonding energy we emit towards ourselves and others. We might think of Gulas Walps's praise and affirmations to Kolin as Gyamkian emissions of this bonding energy that brings us closer and makes us brighter.

To provide some conceptual tools and skills to harness this bonding power, we draw here on a few global thought leaders working in the fields of psychology, social work, medicine, and trauma recovery. We believe this is in keeping with the Truth and Reconciliation Commission's position that "reconciliation is not about 'closing a sad chapter of Canada's past' but about opening new healing pathways of reconciliation that are forged in truth and justice."[13] In engaging mainstream figures in health and social justice, we hope to bring Gitxsan law and cosmology further into a global exchange of ideas that meaningfully responds to the real-world realities we face.

Given the intergenerational traumas endured from the residential and day schools and the Sixties and Millennial scoop experiences, we think it is vital to consider one of the leading treatment approaches for complex post-traumatic stress disorder (PTSD). Rates of complex PTSD are estimated to be high among Indigenous populations.[14] The problem is that many go undiagnosed, or if they are formally diagnosed do not receive quality treatment due to a shortage in healthcare professionals. U.S. psychologist Janina Fisher is a leader addressing complex PTSD. Informed by the latest in neurobiology and decades of clinical practice, Fisher highlights how cumulative trauma results in the fragmentation of self-experience. Our fight, flight, freeze, fawn, and attach survival responses split into distinct parts, holding implicit memories of past traumas. When triggered later in life, we may find ourselves suddenly blending with a younger part in ways that alter our consciousness and, in turn, lead to problematic coping behaviours and overreactions.[15]

From a Gitxsan perspective, we might think of this fragmented experience of selfhood in terms of the Raven stealing the Sun story.[16] Our mythic figure flies off to the Gitxsan who are still living in darkness, in hopes of trading the ball of light for a good deal on salmon. On his way, though, the ball slips out of his beak and shatters into pieces that become the stars and planets of our solar system. This breaking point can be thought of as the cumulative effect of trauma on our spirits, our inner lights. For many in our House families, settler-colonial realities have shattered our integrated sense of personhood. When this happens, healing becomes a matter of embracing these younger fragmented pieces of ourselves, taking them under our wings, as it were, and giving them the warm understanding they missed out on and still long for.[17] When we do this befriending work, we are on the path of building a secure emotional bond with the core parts of who we are. This, in turn, has the potential of breaking the cycle of parental neglect and abandonment—the legacy of the residential and day schools—and the residual violence that stems from intergenerational trauma.[18]

U.S. social work researcher Brené Brown's recent HBO Max special on mapping out meaningful connection and the emotional language of human experience offers an additional resource in taking care of ourselves. In *Atlas of the Heart*, she outlines three aspects of self-compassion. The first is choosing self-kindness over self-judgment. Rather than criticizing ourselves when we drop the ball, kindness means gently tending to the pain of having made a regrettable decision and being curious about how it happened and learning how to prevent it from happening in the future. The second aspect of self-compassion asks us to see our pain and shortcomings as part of the shared human condition. We do not face life's struggles and stresses alone. Other Gitxsan and non-Gitxsan people have worked through similar problems. The third aspect of self-compassion is being mindful rather than overidentifying with a thought or feeling. A mindful approach is about observing and allowing thoughts and feelings to arise and recede without suppressing, denying, or overidentifying with them. To have compassion for what we are going through first requires radical acceptance of our experience and the situation as it is and as it unfolds. As an internationally renowned researcher on shame and vulnerability, Brown highlights the link between self-compassion and the healing of shame. "Shame is a social emotion," she writes. "Even if I feel it alone, shame is the way I see myself through someone else's eyes. Self-compassion is often the first step to healing shame—we need to be kind to ourselves before we can share our stories with someone else."[19] Reflecting on her own experiences with self-criticism, Brown goes so far as to say that "self-kindness is both more difficult and more revolutionary than we think."[20] We agree. Kindness is the heart of the Gyamkian Revolution.

Finally, the Canadian medical doctor and trauma expert Gabor Maté's five varieties of compassion are helpful in extending kindness to others.[21] He first reminds us that the Latin root for ordinary compassion means "to suffer with" and involves the ability to *be with* those who are struggling and to be *moved* by that awareness. It involves empathy, the ability to understand and relate to the feelings of another. It is the opposite of pity, of looking down on one less fortunate. Compassion instead affirms personal responsibility and equality between people. Secondly, there is the compassion of context—a caring perspective that is curious about the root cause of a person's pain and problems. Much like U.S. neuroscientist Bruce Perry and media icon Oprah Winfrey explain, contextual compassion changes the question from "What's wrong with you?" to the more generous "What happened to you?"[22] This approach remains open to all the dynamics that have shaped a person's life and is grounded in the compassion of recognition that invites us to perceive and appreciate that we are all in the same canoe, "roiled by similar tribulations and contradictions."[23] The compassion of truth further recognizes that pain, far from being an enemy, needs to be courageously faced and processed. Truth and compassion are cousins, Maté says, as compassion allows us to accept hard realities with a sense of safety and hope. All of this moves us into a compassion of possibility in which we can embrace the notion that there is more to each of us than the "conditioned personalities we present to the world, the suppressed or untrammelled emotions we act out, and the behaviours we exhibit"; that what appears impossible "only *seems* so, and that whatever we most need and long for can actualize at any moment."[24] To see in each person the inextinguishable potential for wholeness rather than reducing them to their worst traits or deeds would be for us all, in Maté's words, "a victory worth savoring."[25]

These insights and skills give us new glimmers of what it means to harness our star power today. A power that shines in all cultures and fields of research committed to compassion. A power that shines with all House families committed to healing together. Not all memories are traumatized. There are many memories that shine bright; Gyamkian glimmers of a better story. As when grandparents hugged up and pinch the chubby cheeks of grandkids:

"'Wii do'o!" they exclaim. Big cheeks.

Or when the youngest in the Wilp make devil's club medicine necklaces as a way of protecting their aunties and uncles out protecting the lax'yip. Or whenever our cousins induce belly laughter with their colour commentaries on Gitxsan country life or share their stories of spicing up their hagwil jam soup in the city. At such times we feel our star power swell in our very solar plexus, which is the main point of this chapter. Our light and the source of our light cannot be confined to a single tradition, interpretation, or experience. We carry it with us, in the place where the oots'in resides and our spirit flutters alive like a pair of fabled Raven wings gliding us forward with a sense of ease that a new day is possible and, yes, where a good deal on salmon can finally be had and savoured.

7

GWIL WADA/ WILPSTA TALENTS

> In Kispiox when they have what we know today as talent show. Then the white man, the Government closed it down. They didn't want people to do it anymore.
>
> —*X̱hliimlax̱ha*[1]

X̱hliimlax̱ha (Martha Brown) speaks of how we honoured the best and brightest in our House families at talent shows. The talent of one reflected the talent of all in the House and so gwil wada, an exemplary person we might collectively call wilpsta talents, were worth showcasing to the world. At the same time, X̱hliimlax̱ha calls out the historical and ongoing efforts of the Crown to sideline our people from sharing their gifts. It is a government position that has become internalized over the past two centuries. For instance, one of the common things we see and hear happening at meetings between Gitxsan family leaders and industry proponents is the perpetual "capacity funding" offer. Money to do more research on the impact of pipelines on salmon, even though we already have young people like biologist Luu'maja (Taylor Wale) and the Lax'yip Firekeepers who have done the fieldwork to definitively say that such projects will be detrimental to the salmon population. Money to train our people before they can run a child and family services program, even though House matriarchs have been offering this support informally to their loved ones for decades. In short, money premised on the belief that we do not have the know-how to make informed decisions on behalf of our Houses and our territories. We simply reject this deficit model of talent as colonial propaganda.

To counter this trend, we reaffirm a House-centric understanding of individual talents. Every Wilpster has something special to offer the House, the clan, the territory, and the feast. Every Wilpster is responsible for promoting the growth and development of their House's individual and collective capacities. To fulfill these callings, we need to first identify the special abilities of each Wilpster and how these aptitudes can be harnessed to serve the House family's needs. Then we can determine how individual talents can be combined to create a synergy of solar-powered Wilps that exceed what one person can ever do alone. If we do not make this a top priority, we are at risk of losing the cohesion and contributions needed to govern ourselves as lawful people. One way of scouting and retaining our best and brightest is to reimagine the talent show for our times. We call it the Order of Gyamk.

Celebrating Gyamkian Revolutionaries

We believe Gitxsan people deserve a talent show that celebrates and supports those who are doing their best to contribute to the world we live in and keep our legal order alive. The Order of Gyamk can provide the financial aid necessary not just to "build" capacity but to enhance the ability that's already there towards further excellence. It can also serve as a formal means of coordinating across House families to educate everyone about the major initiatives undertaken by Wilpsters on behalf of all. Wilpsters of all ages and backgrounds may be nominated by their peers with House leaders coming together to deliberate and select the front-runners. The awards could then be presented at a feast event that invites all to enjoy an evening of learning based on the latest House achievements in the humanities, sciences, and civic engagements. In what follows, we detail these three broad categories, focusing on the most pressing needs in each. We call on all Wilpsters to use their unique gifts to advance these distinct Gitxsan fields of inquiry and action for the benefit of present and future generations.

The Gitxsan Humanities

The staple Gitxsan humanities consist of Gitxsanimx̲ (the ancestral language), ant'imahlasxw (literature), adaawk (history), sag̲ag̲ootxws (philosophy), and ama'mas g̲ant naxnox (fine arts and performance).

Of these, we believe the Gitxsanimx̲ language is the most essential to revitalize in both the eastern gigeenix and the western gyeets dialects.

According to Gitxsan language researcher Gilga'tsee'ixs (Cheyenne Gwa'amuuk), 5 percent of the Gitxsan population are fluent speakers, 6 percent are semi-fluent, 8 percent are active learners, and 81 percent are believed to be neither speakers nor learners of the language.[2] Drawing on linguist and activist Joshua Fishman's eight-stage scale for reversing endangered language trends, she places her House family in stage seven. This stage is characterized by speakers being mostly over the age of sixty, with language being heard primarily at cultural events, only a few learners, and no children being raised in the language. To revitalize the language at this stage involves engaging Elders as active teachers, strengthening bonds between speakers and learners, creating opportunities for learners to speak and hear the language, training second-language speakers of childbearing age, and bringing the language into the home. Gilga'tsee'ixs reiterates that it "is only possible for languages to reach a healthy state if the language is being used in the home."[3] To this end, she has designed a website that makes Gitxsanimx̱ language resources accessible and offers learning opportunities that could contribute to second-language speakers and the sharing of Gitxsanimx̱ in the home.[4] This digital resource is an especially helpful tool for Wilpsters who live in cities or otherwise away from their villages and so may not have access to a fluent Elder or teacher. In the village of Gitanmaax, Xsiwis (M. Jane Smith) has done much work to revive Gitxsanimx̱ with her grassroots language books and classes.[5] There are many other wilpsta talents like Gilga'tsee'ixs and Xsiwis willing to learn and teach Gitxsanimx̱. We need more of them to keep Gitxsanimx̱ alive.

Advances in Gitxsan literature, history, and philosophy are important in both Gitxsanimx̱ and English translations, in both ancient and new iterations. We envision this humanistic caretaking and creating to be best undertaken by wilpographers—Gitxsan writers, thinkers, researchers, artists, and curators who draw on their own House's unique blend of stories, oral histories, crests, and ideas for inspiration and guidance in thinking about and narrating the times we face today. In terms of new works, we highlight the need for gendering and queering the literary, historical, and philosophical canons so that the voices of Gitxsan girls, women, and Gitxsan people who identify as Two-Spirit, lesbian, gay, bisexual, transgender, queer, questioning, intersex, asexual, and/or gender diverse or nonbinary (2SLGBTQQIA) can be fully amplified and heard. This includes supporting 2SLGBTQQIA scholars and artists studying Gitxsan historical figures and crafting characters reflective of these identities and experiences in their respective narrative accounts.

We also picture Gitxsan artists playing a vital role in the repatriation and innovation of songs, dances, and crest designs that record House histories on button blankets, bent boxes, headdresses, rattles, drums, paddles, canoes, longhouses, and carved poles, among many other artistic objects owned and used by House families today. We especially emphasize the need for a new generation of master carvers to help reincarnate the feasting tradition of pole raising for the twenty-first century. In the last century, anthropologists offered their commentary on the state and condition of our carved poles. While recognizing the Gitxsan had one of the best standing collections along the northwest coast, Marius Barbeau declared that the art form "belonged to the past."[6] Then Haxbagwootxw (Arthur McDames) came along to keep the tradition alive. When Haxbagwootxw entered his later years, Wilson Duff suggested that since McDames did not appear to be training any youth to take his place, he was "probably the last of the Gitksan carvers."[7] Then Geel (Walter Harris) and Delgamuukw (Earl Muldoe) from the fireweed and frog Houses of Anspayaxw stepped up and kept the cedar art form going. Building on their legacies, we need another generation of carving wilpsta talent to once again prove the anthropologists of yesteryear wrong.

Taken together, it is the language speakers, wilpographers, and artists who are the Gyamkian Revolutionaries of the Gitxsan humanities. At the cutting-edge of legal culture, they are the luminaries who make a new day possible.

The Gitxsan Sciences

Gitxsan scientists are those who pair science, technology, engineering, and mathematics with wilpographic knowledge to guide how we care for our ancestors, people, and all species living on the Lax'yip (territories), in the aks g̲ant laxha (water and sky), and through haldaakws (medicine).

In terms of taking care of our ancestors, many of the ancient sites and animals referenced in Gitxsan oral histories have yet to be fully explored by archeologists and paleontologists. This is largely due to the dynamics of coastal environments at the Pleistocene-Holocene transition point approximately 12,000 to 10,000 years ago. As adopted Gitxsan anthropologist Tax'niibaxw (Heather Harris) explains, "Even where the archaeological record exists on the northern Northwest Coast, the record is meager. The convoluted shorelines, rugged landscape and dense vegetation make it difficult to find sites. Most archaeological research has concentrated on the accessible shoreline areas, neglecting other kinds of possible habitation sites. Because of the huge area to survey and the difficulty of access, Wallace Olson contends that the archaeology of the region "is still in its infancy."[8] As an example, Gitxsan geographer Madiigam Gyamk (Neil J. Sterritt) notes that there is still "no concrete evidence for Temlaham's existence."[9] To account for this gap, he suggests that the gullies running through the fields in the area may mark "earlier, deeper and wider river channels." If so, the ancient city "may have been built on what became a floodplain."[10] Only field research can test and ultimately determine the validity of the Madiigam Gyamk hypothesis.

In addition to Temlaxam, oral histories speak of other ancient villages on the coast such as Kadu and Ts'a'os, Gitangasx, Dam Duutsxwhl Ax, and Anlagasemdeex. None have been archaeologically investigated to date.[11] Additionally, oral histories appear to feature extinct megafauna, including giant beaver, dire wolves, American lions, large shellfish, and large alligator-like reptiles. Paleontologists have likewise yet to search out the remains of these ancient species.[12] All this to say, we need an earnest generation of Gitxsan archaeologists and paleontologists working together to unearth the full story of our ancestors.

In terms of taking care of our people, we have seen in Chapter 5 how bush medicine like huu'umst saved Gitxsan lives by treating tuberculosis and rheumatic diseases. Yet to date there is only one book-length manuscript on Gitxsan plant life, completed by the Canadian archaeologist Harlan I. Smith, and it dates back to the 1920s.[13] We need Gitxsan botanists, pharmacologists, physicians, and clinical psychologists, among other health professionals, to work together to determine the therapeutic index of our plant medicines and help define and administer optimum dosages that supplement the best treatments for the intergenerational traumas and related illnesses experienced by our people across the lifespan.

Finally, we call on Gitxsan scientists from all backgrounds to design and implement alternative sources of energy to support sustainable living on the territories and protect species that may be endangered by proposed resource extraction projects. In this respect, Gitxsan computer scientists and engineers may contribute the latest in artificial intelligence and robotics to enhance ecological mapping, transportation, and the safety and security of the territories. Beyond taking care of our planet, we need Gitxsan theoretical physicists to translate ancestral stories of alternate universes into mathematical models and theories and Gitxsan astronomers and astronauts to explore and study the Gyamkian cosmos for habitable zones and intelligent life.

Gitxsan Civic Engagements

The core Gitxsan civic engagements occur at the Wilp (House), Pdeek (Clan), Yukxw (Feast), and Ayookxw (Law) points of inter-Wilp political solidarity and economic partnership. These spheres often overlap and reciprocally shape each other across generations, amounting to a living legacy of Gitxsan ambassadorship to the world.

Take, for instance, the last three generations of leaders within the fireweed House of Gyetm Maxmagii. Hanamuxw (Geoffrey Johnson) was instrumental in abolishing the Canadian legislation that prohibited Indigenous peoples from attending postsecondary schools. His successor and niece, Joan Ryan, was the first person in the family to benefit from the reform and attend university. For her part, she not only completed her teaching degree but further helped establish the Native Indian Teacher Education degree program at the University of British Columbia.[14] She spoke of her diplomatic activism as the work of combining her Gitxsan values with other cultures "to make it stronger" not only for Gitxsan people but for all peoples, "because you work towards a common goal, and the stronger that you can make your commitment to achieve that goal the better it is for you and also for them."[15]

Following in his sister's footsteps, the current Hanamuxw (Don Ryan) organized the *Delgamuukw-Gisday'wa* court action from the 1970s to the late '90s as the president of the Gitxsan-Wet'suwet'en Tribal Council.[16] Through various media platforms, he educated the world on the Gitxsan and Wet'suwet'en peoples' House-based form of democratic governance.[17] Throughout the decades, the House of Gyetm Maxmagii has also supported the work of leading Gitxsan researchers and scholars across disciplines, including education scholar and language teacher Xsiwis (Jane Smith); anthropologist Tax'niibaxw (Heather Harris); and Gyooksgan (Val Napoleon), Governor General

Gold Medal award winner for her work on Gitxsan legal theory, founding director of the Indigenous Law Research Unit, and the first Indigenous woman to serve as dean of the University of Victoria's Faculty of Law.[18]

Alongside these civic-minded wilpsta talents, we honour Cindy Blackstock from the fireweed House of Geel as a major Gitxsan ambassador of the times. Her work over the past twenty-five years in child protection and Indigenous children's rights has garnered her numerous awards, honorary doctorates, and international acclaim. She has collaborated with Indigenous leaders around the world to assist the United Nations Committee on the Rights of the Child in the development and adoption of a General Comment on the rights of Indigenous children. She has worked with Indigenous young people, UNICEF, and the United Nations Permanent Forum on Indigenous Issues to produce a youth-friendly version of the United Nations Declaration on the Rights of the Child. Her promotion of culturally based and evidence-informed solutions has been recognized by the Nobel Women's Initiative, the Aboriginal Achievement Foundation, Frontline Defenders, and many others. She continues to research and teach at McGill University as a professor in social work.[19]

Finally, we honour all the Simgigyet, the hereditary chiefs, who defended our ownership and jurisdiction over our territories as ambassadors to the Crown at the *Delgamuukw-Gisday'wa* trial. In 1994, Hanamuxw (Don Ryan) issued a press release that shared how our hereditary chiefs "had trusted their lives and beliefs to a court that showed no respect for the culture of the Gitksan and the Witsuwit'en." He notes that "by the time our dreams have been realized, many more of our Elders will have died without being awarded the respect and justice they deserve."[20] For their many contributions to the Gitxsan humanities, sciences, and civic engagements on our behalf, we give our Elders the deepest respect and justice they deserve with the long overdue Order of Gyamk.

Following in the footsteps of these humanitarians, we believe the most pressing civic engagements need to be led at the House level with a caring generation of Gitxsan family leaders, social workers, teachers, genealogists, multimedia specialists, diplomats, economists, and business and legal professionals who help clarify the lineages of each House family, facilitate the necessary adoptions so that all Wilpsters may enjoy the rights and privileges afforded by dual clan citizenship, and restore the clan governance system to legitimately mediate and resolve outstanding conflicts within and between Houses along the northwest coast. Beyond the Pacific coastline, Gitxsan athletes at the national and Olympic levels of competition can play vital roles as ambassadors in their chosen sports, and especially so when they use their platforms to broadcast important social and political messages to the world.[21]Taken together, these three award categories orbit around the warm-hearted cosmic ethos concerned with growth in all varieties of life on Earth and are aimed at educating and institutionalizing the Law of Gyamk at the grassroots level. Even at the proposal stage, it raises questions for all Wilpsters to personally consider: What are your gifts and talents? What are you most passionate and curious about in the world? What is your special calling, the creative vocation that only you can take up and realize? What do you plan to contribute to your House in your lifetime? What supports and resources do you need from your House to achieve your goals and dreams? And when you dare to look back on your entire life's work, all the decisions and pathways taken, all the relationships formed over the decades, what do you most want to be known for? How will your life and legacy have impacted the next generation of Wilpsters and the intergenerational project of staying alive as lawful Gitxsan in this awe-inspiring universe?

To reflect long and hard upon such questions, to cultivate a growing sense of the answers your life offers, to take up the long and sweaty labour of bringing your vision into reality, however many setbacks you might face and however far you ultimately get in reaching the peak of your pursuits on behalf of your people and all peoples, may you rest content in knowing your light is a labour of Wilp love most deserving of the Order of Gyamk.

PART 3

GIT'FIT TRAINING

8

SIMGIGYET/ THE FITTEST GITXSAN ON EARTH

> Spookw of Gitanmaax spoke and this is what he said. Great Chief Hanamuxw, I have heard what you said and I have seen myself what you have done. And I can say that while I, like yourself, am young and am learning more about my responsibilities, you have acted before us—you have set before us a good example and your words of wisdom clearly show that your training has also been good.
>
> I shall tell all my people what you have done and what you have said and they shall know everything.... Perhaps we are now in a new generation.... And we have been letting many of the important things of our rights go just through neglect and want of proper training. So, Chief, what I have seen today and heard I will remember and will endeavor to also carry out my position as you are yours.
>
> *—Spookw (Johnson Alexander) as cited in Anderson and Halpin,* Potlatch at Gitsegukla, *177*

The words of Spookw (Johnson Alexander) were written down by our wolf clan relative Gusgai'in (William Beynon) at a pole-raising feast hosted by Hanamuxw (Geoffrey Johnson) in the western village of Gitsegukla on 14 January 1945. As a wolf witness from the eastern village of Gitanmaax, Spookw was commending Hanamuxw for his work on returning their family's pole from Hazelton back to Gitsegukla after the 1936 Skeena River flood.

"Now before I sit," Spookw continued, "I will call on my people from Hazelton who will sing a song in appreciation of your hospitality, and the hospitality of all the chiefs of Gitdzagúk'la."[1]

The song was improvised to express how Hanamuxw had lifted the burdens off their hearts and how they would remember their walk together. In this way, all the Simgigyet, the House family leaders, of Gitsegukla were honoured. This exchange is important to heed for our times as it demonstrates how, differences aside, Simgigyet from all villages stood up to support and inspire each other to be the fittest Gitxsan on Earth.

At the same time, Spookw's remarks about the need for "proper training" raises the spectre of a century-plus breakdown in preparing the youth to take on their responsibilities as the future Simgigyet. In our conversations with the current Hanamuxw (Don Ryan), we have come to appreciate the colonial origins of this breakdown. Before spearheading the *Delgamuukw-Gisday'wa* court action, Hanamuxw worked as a grassroots genealogist and social worker. In his decades serving in these roles, he has seen firsthand how House families have been devastated by the Crown abduction of their children through the residential and day schools and the Sixties and Millennial scoops. "With children removed it all collapsed," he tells us. "Intergenerational conversations, language, memory, the training. It's all missing. People are lost. We are still in that collapse."[2] To rebuild our legal order, Hanamuxw speaks of the Law of Gwelx ye'ent, which he defines as the work of "leaving a functioning House and territory for future generations." It requires each House and its Simgigyet to protect their people and the spirit in their land.

To this end, we reincarnate the "east meets west" Spookw-Hanamuxw tradition of training by drawing on the wisdom of the Gyetm Maxmagii family once again. We return to the words shared at trial by Hanamuxw (Joan Ryan) and Gwaans (Olive Ryan) along with the lessons we've learned from their present leader to detail the democratic culture and compassionate mentorship we need to be the fittest Gitxsan on Earth, family leaders of our Houses and caretakers of our territories.

We Are All Simgigyet

"We are all Simgigyet," Hanamuxw (Don Ryan) teaches us, "We are born into a chiefly culture."[3] Hanamuxw first learned of this ethic from his Elders. Even though he was the youngest of eleven and his oldest sister Joan was being trained as the next Hanamuxw, he remembers the Elders of Gitsegukla still calling him "Sim'oogit Don" as a boy. They affirmed his innate leadership potential, and he lived up to it throughout his life in whatever role and responsibility he was entrusted with, so much so that he was ready to carry on his sister's work when she passed in 2007. Over the last fifteen years, whenever he speaks on behalf of his House in the Feast Hall, he does not give the conventional address that ranks people in terms of male chiefs, high-ranking women chiefs, and children of chiefs. Instead, Hanamuxw greets everyone on equal terms:

"Simgigyet, Simgigyet, Simgigyet."[4]

We are all leaders in his eyes.

The Gyamkian Revolution grows out of this democratic spirit as this chiefly culture guarantees equality among Wilpsters under Gitxsan law and legal order. Whether born or adopted into a House, all Wilpsters hold the same rights and responsibilities. The Law of Gwelx ye'ent does not allow for treating adopted Gitxsan people as second-class citizens. In fact, such treatment contradicts tradition and reality. For one, adoption follows the Gitxsan law known as ts'imil guut. It has been practised by our people over many millennia to protect and enrich the well-being of all.[5] For instance, it was only through the practice of adoption that families like the fireweed House of Gitluudaahlxw and the frog House of Lelt were able to repopulate and rebuild after epidemics like smallpox decimated their numbers. What's more, we cannot overlook the major contributions of Gyooksgan (Val Napoleon) and Tax'niibaxw (Heather Harris), among other adopted Gitxsan people today who have helped rebuild the knowledge base of our lineages and legal orders. In keeping with the rights afforded by ts'imil guut, adoption does not disqualify one from being a family leader.

If we are all born to lead as Simgigyet, then we are all fit to learn and grow in knowledge as Simgigyet. The Gyamkian Revolution calls for the full and transparent sharing of knowledge and experience between all Wilpsters. At trial, Hanamuxw (Joan Ryan) spoke of this as part of the wilksiwitxw teaching tradition: "Our wilksiwitxw is responsible not just in training the chiefs but also the other members of my family. Our wilksiwitxw has a responsibility of ensuring all the members in my immediate family have the same knowledge as I have."[6] As her brother shares with us today, "Training is about raising the ayookxw niyee consciousness in everyone and everything. The consciousness in the songs, in the land, in the medicines, in the oral histories. Whether working in the academy or engaging the Crown, you have to learn to be wilksiwitxw in all places and with all people."[7]

Hanamuxw (Don Ryan) teaches this is an especially important point in light of how settler-colonialism maintains a consciousness industry. It has always sought to shape what we know, how we think about ourselves, and how we relate to each other and the world. Historically, it divided us and imposed a violent assimilation. Today, it occurs more by choice when we lose ourselves in a toxic colonial-capitalist culture as individual consumers and producers. Git'Fit training is firstly an unlearning of colonial forms of consciousness. Clearing ourselves of all mental, emotional, spiritual, and physical toxins so we can then invest our time and energy in learning as much as we can about ayookxw niyee to awaken and feed our Gitxsan legal consciousness. Living in this lucid awareness is the true mark of future leaders and their trusted mentors. Hence, we need to take a closer look at what blocks us from training together like this today.

Training is Quality Time

When we asked Hanamuxw (Don Ryan) what it meant to be trained, he replied unequivocally: "To be trained means 'this is who you need to spend time with.'"[8] Training is quality time with family. For our ancestors, it was always about spending time with their closely related Houses, their wilnadaahl and wilksiwitxw, the people who knew something about their family histories and territories, the ones who imparted the life skills that would help the next generation carry things forward.

Today, we find quality time to be hindered by two realities. Firstly, the Crown systematically sought to destroy our House families and our distinctive wilpographies. There are now many gaps in our knowledge that we have to fill in with the pieces that have survived. This is hard work, but not impossible. There are many texts and multimedia resources that we can use to help us rebuild. Our inter-Wilp collaboration in research and writing has been largely advanced on the archival materials generated by the Simgigyet who shared their knowledge at the *Delgamuukw-Gisday'wa* trial. Spending quality time with publicly available sources, from audio records of language speakers to trial testimonies of our leaders, is a supplemental method of Git'Fit training.[9] It is a method enhanced when paired with House family discussions about these resources and the sisatxw practices of bathing, fasting, and harvesting bush medicine as detailed in Chapter 5.

Secondly, our geographical dispersion from each other and from our territories obstructs our ability to coordinate and train together. It is difficult to think of ourselves as a House family, let alone govern ourselves as such, when we are scattered across British Columbia, Canada, and the United States, among other places we may travel to or reside in for personal or professional reasons. Many Wilpsters are understandably invested in pursuing their careers, enjoying the freedoms of single life, or raising their own families. Training requires time and proximity. Historically, this was not a problem for close-knit families living between their House territories and seasonal village sites. Today, we find our time monopolized by a capitalist economy and our proximity undermined by settler-state geography.

From our research, there are two ways of addressing the Gitxsan diaspora. The first is suggested by Madiigam Gyamk (Neil J. Sterritt). At the end of *Mapping My Way Home*, he encourages all Wilpsters to "welcome the next generation of talented Gitxsan youth and encourage them to stay home or come home and work with the Gitxsan nation."[10] The Madiigam Gyamk solution calls for a grand homecoming of all Wilpsters who find their vocation on our territories. This scale of migration, the likes of which we have not seen since the time of the Temlaxam diaspora, is a big commitment and undertaking that will similarly require 'wii gyamk generous hospitality in the form of housing, employment, and community belonging for all who make the safe return home.

This was the vision the Simgigyet had going into court. As Malii (Glen Williams) spoke of it: "If we had our own land base back what we are making a statement in this court with . . . the chiefs and their house would be responsible for providing housing to their own people . . . and dealing with other problems and ensuring that their house members are dealt with and not . . . suffering from social and housing problems that we have today. . . . They would have a good economic return from their territories which is rightfully theirs. That's the solution that we envision. That's the solution that the chiefs discuss extensively."[11] In a post-*Delgamuukw* Dark Age, Madiigam Gyamk calls us to remain true to this vision: "Gitxsan principles and legal traditions are deeply embedded in our culture. These are the constitutional principles by which the Gitxsan long ago were taught to live. We can rebuild our society from these basic values so that the political and economic institutions we create to address contemporary issues rest on that solid foundation."[12]

While the great Madiigam Gyamk migration takes place, there is also the Hanamuxw (Joan Ryan) long-distance strategy of communication and connection. As a teacher working in the city of Prince Rupert, this was Hanamuxw's bread and butter method of governing her House. On the issue of living away from home, she told the court how "part of it is solved by making many phone calls and having a huge telephone bill."[13] In this way, she found additional help from her family "by delegating a lot of my plans to be handled by Gwaans, Maas Gaak, K'amxtsi kaax, if necessary, and they would make the formal arrangements for me and it may require on my part to make trips back to Gitsegukla before the feast but basically the preparation would be handled by K'amxtsi kaax and Maas Gaak . . . I have received a lot of support from Gwis gyen."[14] Hanamuxw further spoke of how Wilpsters outside of her House sent her "courtesy calls" to get her permission to access and harvest foods from her territories.[15] While delegating and governing from afar, she emphasizes the importance of making every effort to be in her mother's and father's villages of Kitwanga and Gitsekugla as much as she can: "Whenever there are activities in those two villages if I can attend them I certainly try and attend them whenever the dates are set. And if I know them sufficiently beforehand then I make every effort to attend the activities that they have in those villages, and as much as possible contribute where I can ideas that might be helpful to them, support them in whatever way I can."[16] Today, the "courtesy call" is practised in the form of FaceTiming, texting, and other social media methods of staying apprised and up-to-date about the latest House and feast business going on back home. Hanamuxw's example shows us that virtual governing and feasting can be done with integrity. Whether at home or abroad, Git'Fit training remains a matter of putting in the time and the sweat.

The Git'Fit Test for Simgigyet

All this to say, who formally determines the next generation of Simgigyet? What are the tried-and-true criteria, the Git'Fit Test, for conferring on Wilpsters the chiefly names and responsibilities that can be held among Gitxsan on Earth? For answers, we return to the mother and daughter duo Gwaans (Olive Ryan) and Hanamuxw (Joan Ryan).

In her testimony, Gwaans spoke of how there had been a long-standing consensus in her House that the successor to her uncle Geoffrey Johnson would be her eldest daughter. In other words, the authority belongs to each person within a House to determine the succession plan for its wam sim'oogit names. In situations where there is disagreement over a successor, Gwaans states, "That's the time when they talk to themselves in a House and talk it over, and they ch[o]ose someone to get the name."[17] In this respect, Joan mentions the meetings that took place between her House and wilnadaahl and wilksiwitxw before she was conferred the name. "Before the day of [Geoffrey Johnson's] funeral there were meetings going on between the Gisk'aast, between my house and the Gisk'aast chiefs, consultation with my wilksiwitxw before a final decision was made as to what was going to be done about the name and the territory."[18] After their deliberations, it was left to the eldest House matriarch, her grandmother Suu 'Wii Gantxw (Ida Moore), to share with Joan the final decision. "She was doing it according to tradition," Joan recalls; "because she's my grandmother she's the one that is outlining to me some of the things that would be expected of me. She was saying that it was my job to carry on the work of Hanamuxw, the work that he has started in improving the lifestyles of the Gitksan people."[19]

There are several rights and responsibilities associated with the wam sim'oogit names. In addition to attending feasts in the villages on behalf of the Hanamuxw family, Joan explains the name grants her the right "to pass judgment on whether Gitksan laws are fulfilled when a name is transferred to a new candidate or a new chief." She continues, "It also gives me veto power if I feel that certain regulations and laws are not being fulfilled. It gives me the right to participate in all ventures . . . that the chiefs would like to undertake. I'll give this land claims court as an example of where I have the privilege of exercising my right to make the decision to be part of this court case."[20]

With these rights come responsibilities to govern democratically. Although there may be occasions when the Simgigyet must make decisions on their own in the best interests of their House family, Hanamuxw (Joan Ryan) insists that "basically speaking, we make our decisions collectively, because that's part of the tradition of the Gitksan law, that consultation has to take place within your own house, it has to take place within your wil'na t'ahl, it has to take place with the other clans . . . at the village level. But you can also go to the other villages too and go through the same process as well. So the network can sometimes be very large or just confined to your own village."[21] The scope of the issue determines the degree of consultation necessary. For example, an issue impacting all Gitxsan Houses and territories would need consultation among all Simgigyet. Hanamuxw clarifies that these consults are "a requirement before you get to the feast hall" as the presence of the Simgigyet at feasts implies "approval of the way the business is conducted."[22]

At feasts, the Simgigyet also hold the responsibility to ensure everything that is said by fellow Simgigyet about their Houses and territories is correct. "There will be times when errors are made in describing some of the territories and if that is the case, then it's the position of the chiefs who are present to indicate that an error has taken place."[23] Hanamuxw explains this amendment can be done at either that feast or at a later one. Whenever it's addressed, she affirms it is "usually the responsibility of the wilksiwitxw to correct that error. He has to point out that mistakes were made, maybe, in describing a corner of the territory or the fishing sites or maybe the traplines or maybe a wrong crest was used. I can just go that far in giving you examples of what may happen."[24]

To fulfill these responsibilities, the Simgigyet need a working knowledge not only of their House but other Houses in their home village and beyond. In her testimony, Hanamuxw teaches that Simgigyet must be especially versed in five areas:

1. the territories, including hunting grounds, berry patches, and fishing sites;
2. fellow Simgigyet, a familiarity with the active leaders in each House;
3. the organization of feasts, including the selection of appropriate gifts, financial budgeting, and coordinating meetings with other chiefs from related Houses prior to the feast;

4. the delegation of authority, especially to wing-chiefs and other Wilpsters in the House; and
5. the ayuks, crests, of the different Houses and clans.[25]

These areas are taught by both the wilnadaahl and wilksiwitxw sides of the House. Given the depth of knowledge and skills required on the part of the Simgigyet, Hanamuxw clarifies that "you don't get it all at once." She adds that her own Gitxsan legal education is a lifelong process: "I wouldn't for one minute pretend that I know all there is to know about our own traditions. Because there are so many things that you have to remember about the different procedures that you use within a Feast hall and certainly how you treat your guests."[26]

This focus on hospitality brings us to the character shared among the Simgigyet. Firstly, Hanamuxw casts light on how the older generation would create the formal and informal situations to test the character of Wilpsters: "The process of selecting the future chief is an ongoing process very much like your education. The elders, who are your teachers, observe you in many situations very much the same way as they observe contestants in a beauty pageant. Some of the situations might be structured just to observe you and see how you handle it or there could be situations that come about naturally and they are there with you and they observe whether you have the necessary qualities that they expect a chief to have."[27]

These qualities are wide-ranging. It starts with integrity. Simgigyet are people who live by their values and principles. They show respect for and carry on the legacy of preceding generations. They accept responsibility for protecting the smallest life forms on their lands. They are sensitive, good listeners, and independent thinkers. They lead by serving others. They can tolerate distress with dignity and are capable of making split-second decisions when necessary. They educate and protect others in need of guidance and direction. They are humble, sensible, cooperative, and courageous.[28] As Hanamuxw (Don Ryan) puts it, the "chiefs should mean what they say, defend their territories and surrender nothing."[29] Or as his sister consolidates the qualities listed above, the Simgigyet should fully "embrace the idea that your job is not only to make things better for your House but also the entire nation and people outside of your nation."[30]

Hlaa niin xsi gyalatxwit dim ant guuhl hii dax gyets dip niye'en. Dim guudinhl wa midim'y ama gya'adihl Lax'yip.

This is the sentence Joan Ryan provided the courtroom when asked what she understood the name of Hanamuxw required of her. It was what her grandmother Suu 'Wii Gantxw shared with her and what her wilksiwitxw reaffirmed on 1 November 1966 when she formally took up her great-uncle's legacy in a Feast Hall filled with fellow Simgigyet. She translates the Gitxsanimx̲ sentence as, "You are the one that has been selected to take the land that was your inheritance, to hold it, and to take care of it."[31] She then proceeds to draw out the far-reaching implications of this Law of Gwelx ye'enst:

> That means the land that your forefathers had, that includes the regalia, that includes the adaawk, that includes the pole, that includes the resources on the land, that includes the name Hanamuxw, and the right to use that name within the Gitksan territory. That means the right to use the authority of the chief. That includes providing leadership for the people, the Gisk'aast as well as the other clans in Gitsegukla. It means preserving the history of the house. It means taking care of the present, and always with the idea that you link it with the future. It means having the right to assist not just the people in your own house, but everyone in your community if they need help. It means going to other levels of authority whenever you need to negotiate with them to take care of the needs of the people, or it may mean going to neighbouring nations and negotiating with them issues that deal with the Indian problems, or it may mean offering suggestions as to how these can be solved, how the problems can be solved. It also means that you as the chief have the responsibility of training the younger members of your family so that all the traditions, all the customs, all the rituals within your house are maintained. So in a sense the chief is also the teacher for the younger people as well as a counsellor, as well as a spiritual leader.[32]

Those who are entrusted to take up this extraordinary calling, and those courageous enough to back them in carrying out their duties on behalf of their Houses, these are the true Simgigyet, the fittest Gitxsan on Earth.

9

HA GWILII YIN/ WALKING GENTLY

Ha gwilii yin: Walk gently, on a soft path
that is covered with eagle down.

—*Xsiwis (M. Jane Smith),*
"Placing Gitxsan Stories," 8

While the last chapter reincarnated the "east meets west" Spookw-Hanamuxw tradition of training, detailing what Git'Fit training continues to be about, in this chapter we outline *how* we each may go about this training. Ha gwilii yin is the peaceful way forward. It is a path grounded in a proven history of resolving conflicts in a manner that ends cycles of harmful behaviour and violence. Eagle down is a symbol of peace among the Gitxsan and Wet'suwet'en. *Xsiisxw* is the Gitxsanimx̱ term that refers to the law governing compensation.[1] G̲awagaani is the name of the settlement feast our ancestors practised to address conflicts between their Houses and with their coastal neighbours according to the principles of xsiisxw.[2] On these occasions, the eagle down was brought in to support and legitimate lasting peace. Hanamuxw (Don Ryan) explains that restitution and compensation, mainly in the form of land in the case of serious harm, remain "key features in any ceremony in which eagle down is used."[3] He further teaches that g̲awagaani required a commitment from all parties to keep the peace until the heart is satisfied, noting the Gitxsan and Wet'suwet'en have "yet to use eagle down in their dealings with the Crown." In 1994, he wrote that we have been "waiting almost two centuries to make peace with the Crown."[4] Three decades later, we are still waiting for the Crown to make restitution for genocide and to negotiate a meaningful g̲awagaani agreement that compensates for the massive harm it inflicted on generations of Gitxsan and Wet'suwet'en lives, House families, and territories. In a proposal dated January 2023 addressed to the province of British Columbia, Hanamuxw estimates that approximately 50 to 60 percent of the gwelx ye'enst protection work done by the House families on their territories since the last deglaciation period is gone forever, due mostly to large-scale forestry projects, industrial roads, and clear-cut land use.[5] Linear development and losing high-value lands to settlement has accelerated the loss in the last fifty years. He calls for each House territory to be declared a Cumulative Healing Zone to allow for the highly impacted forests and waters to rest and heal. The honour of the Crown demands provincial and federal accountability in this healing process. Hanamuxw is still awaiting meaningful commitment.

What this tell us is that we cannot wait for the Crown to participate in g̲awagaani nor can we overlook how we are implicated in intergenerational cycles of trauma and violence. We are responsible for changing ourselves and the situations we face for the better. What we have learned from Simgigyet from the last chapter is that true transformation is not an individual affair. It does not actualize on sheer willpower alone but with the inspiration and support of many. Facing painful realities, we believe the g̲awagaani tradition offers a Gyamkian source of inner peace that can help us understand and transform our actions within a larger political and legal framework that links us with the efforts of our ancestors as well as the efforts of all those living today committed to meaningful change.[6] As Hanamuxw puts it, "Eagle down gives us optimism. We have kept the eagle down for thousands of years because it works. Eagle down is our law."[7]

In this spirit, we aim to reincarnate the g̲awagaani tradition into a shared grammar of lawful living. This entails applying the principles and precedents of formal peace agreements in our House histories to the daily situations and systems we face today. This work of translating g̲awagaani to the real world adds up to a personal training in the path of eagle down. Each Wilpster and each House has their own understanding and experience of this path. Here we study and reflect on the understandings articulated by the Simgigyet of our families, X̲hliimlax̲ha (Martha Brown) and Antgulilbix (Mary Johnson). Respecting our great-grandmothers, we commit to a lasting peace in a manner that strives to permanently end child abuse, gender-based violence, sexual violence, and lateral violence in our lifetimes.

Gawagaani and the End of Child Abuse, Gender-Based Violence, and Sexual Violence

On 19 September 1985, with the help of Gitxsan translator Frances Sampson, eighty-five-year-old Martha Brown provided the history of how her House obtained territory near the headwaters of the Skeena. "Xsiisxw is a settlement to Xhliimlaxha from way back," Sampson translated for the court. "She doesn't know even who he [the person who held the Xhliimlaxha chief name at the time] was or what he looked like but his sister was killed by [a] Stikine. And the settlement for killing that sister, that territory was given to him."[8] Martha Brown goes on to detail the context of the murder. "They were hunting groundhogs when it happened. They were fixing groundhog to eat. The woman was married to the Stikine side. There may have been jealousy. That's why the man killed her."[9] After the death, she explains that the Stikine man "stuck her in a groundhog hole with a child still on her back."[10] While the House of Xhliimlaxha "found out about her at the time, they never went to take the body. The Stikine people themselves burned it."[11] Then, Martha Brown says, a half-decade later or so, "the Stikine people came out to a place called Xsa'angexhlast [located in the Kispiox Valley] and this is where they turned the territory over to Xhliimlaxha."[12]

She recounts how a Stikine person came to Xsa'angexhlast with a fistful of eagle down in his left hand and a shotgun in his right.[13] "He placed the peace feathers on Xhliimlaxha's head. If Xhliimlaxha brushes the peace feathers off his head, he will be shot. The person stood for some time waiting to see what would happen." Seeing that he accepted the offer of peace, the Stikine began shouting until their House leader came out. "Then the Chief of the Stikine spoke. He didn't just speak but he shouted out for everyone to hear that Malii rose again and Malii is the ownership of the territory."[14] After the territory was given and received as compensation for the death, Martha Brown states that the "Stikine people held a feast the following day. They sang songs to them." These are known as limx xsiisxw, songs of settlement. At this point in her testimony, she sings one of the peace songs. "After they sang their songs," she goes on to say, "the Stikine Chief took his name off the territory. The name is Malii."[15] From then on, the House of Xhliimlaxha has been "the holder of that land. And," she adds, "every winter strong people go up there."[16]

Among the number of issues raised by Martha Brown's g̲awagaani account, we believe the most important is the safety of women and children. At the National Inquiry on Missing and Murdered Indigenous Women and Girls, Cindy Blackstock and Gyooksg̲an (Val Napoleon) provided their expert witness testimony on the issue. As we mentioned in Chapter 1, Blackstock speaks of how the removal of children into Crown custody is directly related to socioeconomic conditions: "To give you a sense of the scale of it just for on-reserve, between 1989 and 2012, we've known that First Nations kids are 12 times more likely to go into child welfare care, primarily driven by neglect, primarily driven by poverty, substance misuse and by poor housing."[17] To understand the impact of this overrepresentation, Blackstock puts the statistics in terms felt by the children themselves. "How many sleeps did First Nations kids spend away from their families in foster care between 1989 and 2012? And it was 66 million nights, or 187,000 years of childhood."[18] As part of the solution, Blackstock encourages us to "re-embrace those cultural ways of keeping kids safe and [to] be prepared to do that."[19] She goes on to identify what has been taken from us and what we need to restore as House families: "We feel that one of the things taken from many Indigenous Peoples through colonization, perhaps even, I would argue, the most important thing was our ability to dream for ourselves. What does a healthy Gitxsan family and child look like? Some of us have pieces of that vision, but that communal vision, that was broken apart; in some cases, more than in others. And so, one of the first things is to re-dream what that looks like, and then work with community to re-establish that dream."[20] From an Indigenous law perspective, Gyooksg̲an adds that the "issue of missing and murdered Indigenous women and girls is not only a legal issue within Canadian law. It's an issue within our different Indigenous legal orders. And the work of Indigenous law includes that of rebuilding citizenries and rebuilding our lawfulness."[21] To this end, she encourages us to question our own assumptions and raise new questions: "Instead of saying, 'What are the traditional gender roles?' as if they always have to be that way and always were unchanging in the past, we look at how do our understandings about gender and sexuality today shape the way that we work with law and shape our legal interpretations?"[22] Gyooksg̲an speaks of this as more than intellectual work. She asserts we have to invest "the time and the mental work as well as emotional and spiritual work to do that, so that we don't idealize Indigenous law and so that it is capable of dealing with the realities that our communities are living with."[23]

By bringing Martha Brown's g̲awagaani testimony into dialogue with Blackstock and Gyooksg̲an's insights, we are able to dream of a new purpose for the territories near the headwaters of the Skeena. One of the Calls to Justice (no. 7.3) is to create nation-specific healing initiatives that "lift up" Indigenous boys and men.[24] This includes providing safe spaces to discuss emotions, learn healthy coping skills for negative emotions, and learn about healthy relationships and parenting. It also includes building alliances against misogyny and violence against women, such as the recent Moose Hide Campaign; mentorship programs and male role models to promote healthy forms of masculinity; networking and employment support services; and culturally grounded on-the-land programs to learn skills such as hunting and fishing.[25]

Taking this Call to Justice to the heart of Gitxsan law and legal order, we dream of winters when strong people make the journey to the headwaters of the Skeena River to lift up Gitxsan boys and men. The land itself holds the story of how jealousy, among other harmful feelings, can lead men to commit violence against women. Wilpsters and matriarchs from our X̲hliimlax̲ha family and related Houses can lead this initiative, teaching the life skills around taking care of our emotions and building healthy relationships with ourselves and others as lawful Gitxsan.[26] It would be a House initiative committed to ensuring no more crimes like the one Martha Brown described ever happen again. This call to justice thus forms part of our Gitxsan legal obligations that reach well beyond Canadian law.[27] We cannot afford to neglect this work. As our father and great-uncle 'Wii Muk'willixw (Art Wilson) reminds us, "we have to deal with these issues or the cycles will never be broken."[28] It is a cycle that is being broken with the kind of Gitxsan parenting and care modelled by Gitxsan journalist Angela Sterritt who, in a personal letter found at the end of her 2023 book *Unbroken*, imparts Gyamkian teachings to her eleven-year-old son Namawan: "Loving yourself, my dear son, is an act of decolonization and resistance. While we have in our recent past been treated as subhuman, I am confident you will love and cherish who you grow up to be as an Indigenous man and treat Indigenous women and girls just the same because we are all rising together, holding our pens of healing, change, and light together as one."[29] Each Wilpster and House family has a part to play in this Gyamkian form of compassionate parenting to the next generation and ourselves. We must commit each day to living in a manner that prepares and conditions us to be family leaders of eagle down.

G̲awagaani and the End of Lateral Violence

On 28 May 1987, Antgulilbix (Mary Johnson) spoke of g̲awagaani principles in relation to the character and responsibilities of Simgigyet. In light of substance abuse problems faced by the community, Antgulilbix explains they look first for a person who "lives a clean life and not an alcoholic because the chief name is so sacred among the Indians, and also the territory, and we want someone that's really wise and understand[s] the laws of our land and respect[s] the rest of the tribe, honour[s] the rest of the tribes."[30]

To be sure, it has always been difficult to find people who meet the highest Simgigyet standards of conduct. Hence, the eagle down has been brought in to guide the selection process. As Antgulilbix explains,

> In the very ancient time grandmother said the chiefs had a hard time selecting a chief. . . . The chiefs [*sic*] life should be clean and pure because . . . the eagle down is white, that means pure and eagle down is soft and—very soft. That's why I say when you are grieved, and the chiefs will speak to you in the Feast House if there's any death in the family, and you could feel their words. . . . It's just like as if the feathers fell on you, on your life, that's how their words are.[31]

She goes on to state the importance of being honest and respectful. She details how this standard extends to all House leaders and their partners. There is no place for guu galamk', gossiping, because, as Antgulilbix says, it "hurt people's feeling, [so] then the chiefs of the House would select another one because they want the chief and the territory to be complete pure and true and the chief is supposed to tell the truth, not to lie about anybody else's territory."[32] This latter point highlights how the whole territorial boundary system relies on honesty. Given the bar that Wilpsters had to reach in order to be selected as trusted successors, it was a celebratory occasion when new Simgigyet were formally recognized in the Feast Hall. As Antgulilbix's fireweed relative, Gwis Gyen (Stanley Williams), explains in his testimony:

> After this happens, then the successor puts all his regalia on and he puts his hat on and on top of his hat he has the sea lion's whiskers, and after when he puts his head wear on and then he puts the eagle down on top of his . . . head wear, and while this is going on the people behind the curtains are singing. And what he does is he comes out jumping, dancing, and he's doing his halayt [dance]. While he's doing this, the feathers are flying out to the head chiefs. He . . . is very happy that the people have c[o]me to the feast, Dii yee'mgyet, and to show this he is dancing and . . . he's giving feathers to show that . . . he has a peaceful mind.[33]

Gyooksgan speaks to the symbolic significance of the eagle down here. She says it is the next generation of Simgigyet confirming they are "properly prepared and trained, mature and thoughtful, and able to fulfill [their] legal and political responsibilities. This eagle down demonstration," she goes on to say, "is also important in that the chief acknowledges the other chiefs and the importance of their relationships to his House and in the fulfillment of his role."[34]

We believe Antgulilbix's gawagaani teachings on the character and conduct of Simgigyet are especially relevant to addressing the lateral violence in our communities. In *Reclaiming Power and Place*, the final report of the National Inquiry on Missing and Murdered Indigenous Women and Girls, lateral violence is defined as "violence directed against one's peers instead of their adversaries."[35] The report identifies how this kind of violence impacts Indigenous communities across the country. "One of the distinctive elements that emerged over the course of the Dialogue sessions was how, for some community members and front-line workers, lateral violence can also contribute to the targeting of individuals for violence."[36] In her feminist research and activist work in Indigenous communities, Gyooksgan has spoken out against lateral violence as Indigenous incivility.[37] She shares personal examples of the problem:

> Recently for example, a friend for whom I have the greatest respect, and who served several years as the elected chief

> of his community, described his experience of being at the receiving end of appalling personal attacks from competing community factions. I know of other fine people who have had similar experiences, many of whom subsequently left their communities so their families could escape these kinds of highly charged and personally destructive attacks. These people are not perfect, but they are committed, knowledgeable and hard-working, and they often have to remove themselves from direct local struggles as a matter of their own survival.[38]

Reflecting upon these troubling realities with Antgulilbix's g̲awagaani principles in mind, we call for the end of Gitxsan lateral violence and incivility in all its forms. There is no place for personal attacks, shaming, or bullying. There is no place for gossip, lies, or ridicule. There is no place for racism, ageism, ableism, sexism, homophobia, or transphobia. We cannot make fun of each other for any reason under the pretenses of toxic "joking." Nor can we inflict this treatment on ourselves as it is this kind of speech and behaviour that erodes our daxgyet and 'wii bil'ust, our power and light, as Wilpsters and as House families.

Whether we hold wam sim'oogit names or not, we are all responsible for offering eagle down to each other. Returning the feathers to our leaders who are not perfect but who are trying their best; returning the feathers to our loved ones who identify as Two-Spirit, lesbian, gay, bisexual, transgender, queer, questioning, intersex, asexual, and/or gender diverse or nonbinary, honouring all their gifts and contributions; and returning the feathers to Gitxsan girls and women, the present and future matriarchs of our Houses. As a Gitxsan legal response to Call to Justice no. 1.8, we commit to helping to advance the Antgulilbix Awareness Campaign in our everyday conversations and relationships to combat all forms of lateral violence in Gitxsan communities today.[39]

From our House matriarchs, X̲hliimlax̲ha (Martha Brown) and Antgulilbix (Mary Johnson), we learn that the great g̲awagaani tradition has always been about facing painful realities together with courage and the deepest understanding and compassion for all sides. It takes time, patience, and lifelong commitment across generations. To do this work is not only worthwhile, it is obligatory under Gitxsan law. Whether it's envisioning and one day leading a land-based healing program to uplift Gitxsan boys and men on X̲hliimlax̲ha's territory or supporting grassroots community campaigns in honour of Antgulilbix's g̲awagaani teachings, these are the real-world initiatives of the Ḡyamkian Revolution. If we wish to break cycles of violence, we cannot neglect these efforts, nor can we fail to draw on the naxnox powers and wilpsta talents; we have to do this work, and do it well. It begins with bathing and fasting and is fuelled by bush medicine, the kind found on the devil's club necklaces our House families wear in solidarity to each other and the Lax'yip. The reincarnational element is all around us. We just have to look for it and keep going.

We hope to have shown here that the path of eagle down, the ha gwilii yin way of lawful living, remains alive today and leads to a peaceful future to the degree we awake each morning to make a new day, one that is free of child abuse, gender-based violence, sexual violence, and lateral violence, among other painful legacies of genocide. As people of eagle down, we are called to fight for the human rights afforded to us all but never in a way that has us fighting with each other. When internal disagreements arise, as they have and will, eagle down must be brought into our hearts and minds. Eagle down is our law.

EPILOGUE

SAGAYT K'I'YHL GAGOODIIT/ UNITY

The vision, unity, solidarity, and accountability of the entire Gitxsan nation—with the tribal council and band councils working together leading up to and during the Delgamuukw case—was critical to the outcome of Delgamuukw. Unfortunately, that unity has not lasted. We have since struggled with internal problems that continue today. The hard reality is that the internal struggles among the Gitxsan have frustrated the advancement of the whole nation toward the goals the case was out to achieve.

—Madiigam Gyamk (N.J. Sterritt),
Mapping My Way Home, *321*

Shortly before his untimely death, Madiigam Gyamk (Neil J. Sterritt) wrote these words at the end of *Mapping My Way Home: A Gitxsan History*, a passionate account of his life's work. "Back in 1956," he tells us like a ye'e, "nine Native Brotherhood of BC Leaders suggested that I attend law school in order to advance the land question." Being a lawyer was not his calling, however, for Madiigam Gyamk had a gift for geography. "That path," he goes on to say, "allowed me to work directly with the *simgiiget* and identify and map the historical territories of the Gitxsan Houses so they would be preserved for all time." His work and those of many in his generation did much to advance human rights for Gitxsan and Wet'suwet'en people. Yet he humbly admits "there is still much to be done." And this work, he reminds his generation, "will fall, as it should, to our children and grandchildren. With our support, they will have the means by which to find their way home."[1]

Madiigam Gyamk's grandfatherly spirit calls each of us to further refine the reincarnation of our laws and legal traditions. This entails that we unite once again as Wilpsters. Whatever generation, House, clan, village, or territory we come from, wherever we may reside, however we make a living, and whatever we believe about the cosmos, we face the same truth: We need each other. In order to take up Git'Fit training, to find that gentle path of ha gwilii yin that can help heal the painful realities we face, we need to come together in that unity that Madiigam Gyamk spoke of.

If we don't, if we neglect to train and practise what we know to be proper and true, if we neglect to talk and share our lives with each other, then it will only be within a generation or two that the enduring legal order we know today—the one that does not rely on the Crown but rather on sixty-plus House families working together in ancient clan and village alliances, the one that dared to tell the world on 12 May 1987 that our Wilp rights and responsibilities to the Lax'yip have not been extinguished and we will continue to govern with or without Crown recognition—*that* legal order will collapse, and we will be Gitxsan only in name rather than in law.[2]

As two Gitxsan cousins and students of ayookxw niyee coming out of the gambling Houses of Git'tsim'gedimgyat and Git'luuhl'um'hetxwit, we have banked our scholarship on the power of our wilpsta talents—that we will wake up, step up, and keep going. As a lawful people, we have exercised this capacity in spades across two glaciation periods and have survived 12,000 years to tell the tale of it all.[3] Together, we can carry on the call and charge of being lawful Gitxsan and so reincarnate the spirits of our ancestors. In this way, we might one day say to each other in a 'wii yukxw, a big feast, with all of us present:

Withl ap ligi aapxin diihl wisim wil sagayt k'i'y ga goot'sim.[4]

It looks like light work with unity.

This 'wii yukxw level of solidarity is built on the everyday connections we make with each other. First in our own Houses and then branching out into our wilnadaahl and wilksiwitxw, making for one big family all across Gitxsan country and beyond. Here, in the language of our ancestors, we encourage each Wilpster to make these sgano connections:

Eda gya'as nigwoodin, ye'en, noo'n gant ts'iits'n!
Eda gya'as nibib'n, nixdaa'n, gant gutxa'oo!
Eda gya'as Simgigyet gant ansipsiipinsxw![5]
Go see your fathers, your grandpas, your mothers, and your grannies!
Go see your uncles, your aunties, and your cousins!
Go see your House leaders and elders and all your loved ones!

Sit and listen and learn as much as you can. Use your eyes and ears. Bear witness to their amazing lives. Share what you have learned and teach what you know. In this way, create the conversations that bring you closer to the core of who you are. This 'wii bil'ust, this star power that is your light and life, is your rightful inheritance imparted to you by the cosmic presence of love our ancestors knew as Gyamk. This is the Law of Gyamk and Gwelx ye'enst. The one spoken of by Delgamuukw (Ken Muldoe) on day one of the Delgamuukw trial: "Together, the Gitksan and Wet'suwet'en Chiefs own and govern the 22,000 square miles of Gitksan and Wet'suwet'en territory. For us, the ownership of the territory is a marriage of the Chief and the land. Each chief has an ancestor who encountered and acknowledged the life of the land. From such encounters come power. The land, the plants, the animals and the people all have spirit, they all must be shown respect. That is the basis of our law."[6] We are in it together, weaving a solid fabric, a sgano that stretches across the sky, one conversation at a time. And so we proclaim:

Wilpsters of the Lax'yip, unite!

’NII DIL/ AFTERWORD

Sim’oogit Hanamuxw (Don Ryan),
on behalf of the Gyetm Maxmagii family

I am Sim’oogit Hanamuxw from the House family of Gyetm Maxmagii of the Gis’kaast/Fireweed Clan, from the ancient village of Tsa Anwokgisxw.

I began my public life as a social worker and genealogist before serving as executive director of the Gitxsan-Wet’suwet’en Tribal Council, leading the court action now known as *Delgamuukw-Gisday’wa*, where the Supreme Court of Canada recognized Aboriginal title as an unextinguished right under the Constitution Act, 1982.

I honour my late mother, Sim’oogit Gwaans (Olive Ryan), and my late sister, Sim’oogit Hanamuxw (Joan Ryan), who testified on ayookxw niyee—the laws of our ancestors. I carry their legacies of wisdom and compassion as the current Hanamuxw, a name held through generations of family leaders who have upheld Gitxsan law since time immemorial.

As a Gisk’aast Sim’oogit from another village, I write this as ’nii dil—a witness from the opposite clan whose duty is to confirm the truth of what has been shared. In our law, such witnessing is a form of ratification: when an opposite-clan Sim’oogit stands as ’nii dil, the words enter collective memory and become part of our living record.

The Gyamkian Revolution is a masterpiece of Gitxsan legal thought and political imagination. It demonstrates our laws continue to evolve through coordinated land defence, scholarship, and the art of relationship. The House families of Git’tsim’gedimgyat and Git’luuhl’um’hetxwit have offered an inspiring vision worthy of critical study in any college or court in this country. It renews an ancient training for our times, reminding us that the law of gwelx ye’enst is alive in every act of stewardship and love for the land.

As Sim'oogit Hanamuxw of the Gis'kaast, I wholeheartedly affirm: These words stand as true. They form part of the continual flow of Gitxsan law and may be relied upon as evidence of our continuing sovereignty and jurisdiction over our territories.

That's Gyamk!

GITXSANIMX̲ GLOSSARY

Term (Language)	Definition / Translation / Contextual Note
Algyah; Algyax (v.) (Gitxsanimx̲)	To speak
Ama'mas g̲ant naxnox (Gitxsanimx̲)	Expression for fine arts and performance; refers to dance, theatre, and spiritual dramatization
Amnigwoot (Gitxsanimx̲)	Privileges held in respect to one's father clan's Lax'yip (Territory)
Amxsiwaa (Gitxsanimx̲)	White; used to describe whiteness or, more recently, European newcomers
Ant'imahlasxw (Gitxsanimx̲)	Literature; includes oral and written works of storytelling and record
Ayookw; Ayook (Gitxsan)	Law; the collective Gitxsan system of governance, custom, and justice
Ayookxw niyee (Gitxsanimx̲)	"The law of our grandfathers"; ancient hereditary law handed down through generations
Ayookxwm Gwelx Ye'enst; Ayoogam gwahlyee'nst (n.) (Gitxsanimx̲)	"The law of inheritance"; hereditary law governing the transfer of names, territories, and duties
Ayuks; Ayukws (Gitxsanimx̲)	Crests representing a Wilp's identity, lineage, and rights
Bax maga gyet (Gitxsanimx̲)	Totem pole raising and associated feast reaffirming hereditary rights
Bil'ust (Gitxsanimx̲)	Star; central to Gitxsan cosmology and history
Daxgyet; Daxgyat (n., v.) (Gitxsan)	Power; spiritual and authoritative capacity aligned with law and ancestral force

Dii yee'mgyet (Gitxsanimx)	Expression of joy or peaceful contentment; often enacted through dance or generosity
Ga jaak (Gitxsanimx)	Rope; may also symbolize connection or binding in metaphorical usage
Gaats (Gitxsanimx)	In-clan marriage; prohibited under Ayookw
Gal gyamk (Gitxsanimx)	Too hot; descriptive phrase
Gawagaani (Gitxsanimx)	Settlement feast for restoring peace between groups
Gigeenix (Gitxsanimx)	Upriver; directional term referring to the upper Skeena region
Git (Gitxsanimx) (prefix)	People; plural of gyat ("person"). Prefix used in Gitxsan
Git'Fit (Gitxsan / English)	Play on "get fit"; denotes the skill or fitness of a Wilpster
Gitxsan: Gitksan (n.) (Gitxsanimx)	Commonly interpreted as "People of the River of Mist." From Git (People), Xsi (River), Ye'en (Mist)
Gitxsanimx (Gitxsan)	The language of the Gitxsan people; part of the Tsimshianic family
Guu galamk' (Gitxsanimx)	To gossip
Gwalgwa (Gitxsanimx)	To dry off
Gwil wada (Gitxsanimx)	Exemplary person; one of moral and social excellence
Gya'am niin (Gitxsanimx)	"I see you"; expression of recognition or greeting
Gyamk(hl) goot'y (Gitxsanimx)	"Heart is full of warmth and happiness"
Gyat (Gitxsanimx)	Singular term for "person"
Gyeets (Gitxsanimx)	Downriver; toward the lower Skeena
Ha gwilii yin (Gitxsanimx)	"Walk softly / gently"; expression of humility and care

Hagwil jam (n.) (Gitxsanimx̱)	"Easy cooking"; referring to a Gitxsan soup dish
Hawal (n., v.) (Gitxsanimx̱)	Collective contributions of a Wilp to cover ceremonial expenses or compensations
Hla ga kaaxhl sim'oogit (Gitxsanimx̱)	A hereditary wing-chief's name
Huu'umst (Gitxsanimx̱)	Devil's club (Oplopanax horridus); sacred medicinal plant
Iinoowhlxw (Gitxsanimx̱)	The baby-naming process involving both the father's and mother's clans
Lagam'yatsa (Gitxsanimx̱)	Feast commissioning totem pole carvers; public recognition of rights and responsibilities
Lahal (Gitxsanimx̱)	Ancient gambling game using bones or sticks, often accompanied by song
Lax'yip (Gitxsan)	Territory; the fundamental land unit managed collectively by a Wilp
Limx oo'y (n.) (Gitxsanimx̱)	Ancient dirge song performed for the deceased
Maalgwasxw (n.) (Gitxsanimx̱)	Indian Hellebore; a plant medicine used in cleansing rituals
Na-muk (Gitxsanimx̱)	Child's name; often carrying ancestral significance
Nax' niin (Gitxsanimx̱)	"I hear you"; expression of acknowledgment or respect
Naxnox; Naxnok; Naknok (n., v.) (Gitxsanimx̱)	Spirit being or power; manifestation of spiritual force
Pdeek (Gitxsanimx̱)	Clan; one of the four Gitxsan kinship divisions
Sagagootxws (Gitxsanimx̱)	Philosophy; the worldview and ethical thought of the Gitxsan
Sagayt k'i'yhl gagadiit/ goot (Gitxsanimx̱)	"To be among one heart"; expression of unity and collective purpose

Sbil Naxnox (Gitxsanimx̲)	Place of supernatural or spiritual significance, tied to a specific naxnox
Sgano (Gitxsanimx̲)	Woven fabric; metaphor for social cohesion and interconnection
Sii halayt (Gitxsanimx̲)	Baby name ceremony; conferral of names for newborns
Sim'oogit (n.) (Gitxsan)	Hereditary chief or leader responsible for the well-being of a Wilp
Sisatxw (n., v.) (Gitxsanimx̲)	"Making a new day"; purification or renewal ritual
T'ooyaxs'y niin (Gitxsanimx̲)	"I thank you"; expression of gratitude
Tee'ts; t'ets; t'its (n., v.) (Gitxsanimx̲)	Messengers sent to invite other houses to a Yukxw (Feast)
Wam sii halayt (Gitxsanimx̲)	New dancer name; bestowed in dance or ceremonial initiation
Wam sim'oogit (Gitxsanimx̲)	A hereditary chief's name
'Wii do'o (Gitxsanimx̲)	"Big cheeks"; from 'wii (big) and do'o (cheek); term of endearment
'Wii gyamk generous (Gitxsan / English hybrid)	Play on sui generis; Gitxsan critique of colonial "Aboriginal title" concept
Wilksiwitxw; wilsiwitxw (Gitxsanimx̲)	One's father's clan
Wilnadaahl; Wil'naat'aahl (Gitxsanimx̲)	Closely related houses of one's mother's clan
Wilp li'ligit (Gitxsanimx̲)	Feast hall; central institution of Gitxsan governance
Wilpography (English / Gitxsan hybrid)	Study of one's Wilp; interdisciplinary research into one's house and relations
Wilpster / Wilpsta (English / Gitxsan hybrid)	Citizen of a Wilp; modern term derived from "hipster"

X'yansxw (Gitxsanimx̲)	Tuberculosis; a dangerous ailment introduced through colonization
Xhluuhligyootxw (Gitxsanimx̲)	Axe; tool gifted to assist in totem pole construction
Xsi (Gitxsanimx̲)	River, waterway, or creek
Xsiisxw (Gitxsanimx̲)	Law of compensation; principle of balance and restitution
Xsinaahlxw (Gitxsanimx̲)	Breath song; sacred invocation of life and continuity
Yenk; Yankw (n.) (Gitxsanimx̲	Mould
Yukxw; Yuxw (n., v.) (Gitxsanimx̲)	Feast; central political and legal institution where law and history are affirmed

Name	Contextual Note
Anlagasemdeex; Anlagasimdeex	Ancient ancestral village; no longer inhabited
Anspayaxw	Gigeenix (Upriver) Gitxsan village at the confluence of the Kispiox and Skeena Rivers
Antgulilbix	Hereditary name of the Git'luuhl'um'hetxwit, a Fireweed Clan house from Anspayaxw
Anxya'gen	Creek located north of Anspayaxw
Dam Duutsxwhl Ax	Ancient ancestral village; no longer inhabited
Delgamuukw	Hereditary name of Wilps Delgamuukw; a Frog Clan house from Anspayaxw
Delgamuukw–Gisday'wa Court Case	Refers to the 1997 Gitxsan–Wet'suwet'en title case
Dimdiigibuu	Hereditary name of Wilps Gutginuuxw, a Fireweed Clan house from Anspayaxw
Gawa Gyanii	Hereditary name of Wilps Gwinuu, a Frog Clan house from Gitanyow
Gilga'tsee'ixs	Hereditary name of Wilps Wosim Laxha, a Fireweed Clan house from Anspayaxw
Gisday'wa	Wet'suwet'en hereditary name of the Wolf Clan
Gisk'aast	Fireweed Clan
Gitangasx	Ancient ancestral village; no longer inhabited
Gitanmaax (english); Git-an'maaxs (n.)	Upriver Gitxsan village at the confluence of the Bulkley and Skeena Rivers
Gitanyow; Gitanyaw	Gyeets (Downriver) Gitxsan village south of Kitwancool Lake near the Kitwanga River

Gitdzagúk'la / Gitsegukla; Gijigyukwhla	Gyeets (Downriver) Gitxsan village at the confluence of the Gitsegukla and Skeena Rivers
Gitluudaahlxw	Hereditary name of Wilps Gitluudaahlxw, a Fireweed Clan house from Anspayaxw; Closely related to the Git'luuhl'um'hetxwit
Git'luuhl'um'hetxwit	Fireweed Clan house from Anspayaxw; name means "People in the Front Standing"
Git'tsim'gedimgyat	Wolf Clan house from Anspayaxw; means "People of the Fastened Man"
Gusg̱ai'in	Hereditary name of a Nisg̱a'a Wolf Clan house
Gwaans	Hereditary name of Gyetm Maxmagii, a Fireweed Clan house from Gitsegukla
Gwalx luu wan	Ear-piercing hereditary name of the Git'luuhl'um'hetxwit; meaning "They all come out dancing together"
Gwashl Am	Hereditary name of Wilps Gwashl Am, a Wolf Clan house from Gitanyow
Gwaxskiik / Kwarxkik	Hereditary name of Git'tsim'gedimgyat, a Wolf Clan house from Anspayaxw
Gwiis logam phlo'on	Divorce name of Mary Johnson; meaning "Old white sea-otter blanket"
Gwinuu	Hereditary name of Wilps Gwinuu, a Frog Clan house from Gitanyow
Gwis Gyen	Hereditary name of Wilps Gwis Gyen, a Fireweed Clan house from Gitsegukla
Gyamk	The "Sun Being" and ancestral figure of the Fireweed Clan, from the Adaawk of Ska'wo
Gyetm Maxmagii	Ancestral being and Fireweed Clan house from Gitsegukla (also known as the House of Hanamuxw)

Gyooksgan	Hereditary name of Wilps Luuxhon, a Frog Clan House from Gitanyow; held by scholar Val Napoleon
Hagwilget; Hagwilgyat	Wet'suwet'en village located on Gitxsan territory near New Hazelton, BC
Hak'w (haxxw(?))	Hereditary name of Wilps Hak'w, a Frog Clan house from Kitwanga
Hamiyaahl hloxs	Hereditary name of the Git'luuhl'um'hetxwit; meaning "The Sun is Always Thankful"
Hanamuxw	Hereditary name of Gyetm Maxmagii, a Fireweed Clan house from Gitsegukla
Hawaaw	Hereditary name of the Git'tsim'gedimgyat, a Wolf Clan house from Anspayaxw
Haxbagwootxw	Hereditary name of Wilps Haxbagwootxw, a Fireweed Clan house from Gitsegukla
Hooxi'i	Hereditary name of the Git'luuhl'um'hetxwit, a Fireweed Clan house from Anspayaxw
Kadu	Ancient ancestral village; no longer inhabited
Kaldo'o; Galdo'o (n.)	Gigeenix (Upriver) Gitxsan village near the confluence of the Skeena River and Kuldo Creek
K'amxtsi kaax	Hereditary name of Gyetm Maxmagii, a Fireweed Clan house from Gitsegukla
Keemelay	Ancient village from the Adaawk of Ska'wo
Kisga'ga'as; Gisaga'as; Gisgaga'as (n.)	Gigeenix (Upriver) Gitxsan village on the Babine River
Kitkatla	Tsimshian village located on an island south of Prince Rupert
Kitselas; Gits'ilaasxw	Tsimshian village located on the Skeena River east of Terrace, BC

Kitwanga; Gitwangak; Gitwangax	Gyeets (Downriver) Gitxsan village at the confluence of the Kitwanga and Skeena Rivers
Kuhlarrantu	The half moon, described in the Adaawk of Ska'wo
Kunradal	Ancient village from the Adaawk of Ska'wo
Laa'm gayt	Crest of Gyetm Maxmagii (House), depicting the hat worn by Gyetm Maxmagii (Naxnox)
Laha	Sky; domain of Gyamk in the Adaawk of Ska'wo
Lasimedeek	One of the thirteen Gitxsan moons
Lax Gibuu	Wolf Clan
Lax See'l / Ganada	Frog Clan
Lax Skiik	Eagle Clan
Laxwiiyip; Laax'wiiyip	Ancient village near the headwaters of the Stikine, Nass, and Skeena Rivers
Lax'yip Firekeepers	A youth-led association of Gitxsan from all Gitxsan villages, working toward sustainable futures on the Lax'yip
Ligii yuun	One of the Children of the Sky; figure from the Adaawk of Ska'wo
Luu'maja	Gitxsan hereditary name of Wilps Gwoimtxw, a wolf clan house from Kisgegas; held by the biologist Taylor Wale
Maas Gaak	Hereditary name of Gyetm Maxmagii, a Fireweed Clan house from Gitsegukla
Madiigam Gyamk	Hereditary name of Wilps Gitluudaahlxw, a Fireweed Clan house from Anspayaxw; once held by Neil J. Sterritt, author of *Mapping My Way Home*

Malii	Hereditary name of Wilps Malii, a Wolf Clan house from Gitanyow
Maudeks	Supernatural fountain from the Adaawk of Ska'wo
M'deek / Mediik; Madiik; Madiigam Ts'u'wii'aks	Supernatural Grizzly Bear that once attacked Temlaxam; central figure in the Adaawk of Temlaxam
Naga'ihl	Hereditary name of the Git'luuhl'um'hetxwit, a Fireweed Clan house from Anspayaxw; and an ancestor referenced in the Adaawk of the Git'luuhl'um'hetxwit
Neas Hiwas; Niis'hawas	Fireweed Clan ancestor and hereditary name from Temlaxam
Neas-D-Hok; Niistaxo'ok; 'Niisdahukw	Hereditary name of a Fireweed Clan house from Kitselas
Nii'lax Aks	Hereditary name of the Git'luuhl'um'hetxwit, a Fireweed Clan house from Anspayaxw
Nisga'a	Neighbouring and ancestral relative of the Gitxsan, located around the mouth of the Nass River
Nits'iits Ska'wo	"Grandmother of Ska'wo"; figure from the Adaawk of Ska'wo
Sagayt ga'ak	Hereditary name of the Git'luuhl'um'hetxwit, a Fireweed Clan house from Anspayaxw; and an ancestor referenced in the Adaawk of the Git'luuhl'um'hetxwit
Sagayt 'na lo'ixsxw	Baby name meaning "The bear cubs stay in their den during wintertime"; once held by Mary Johnson
Sikedakhl	Gigeenix (Upriver) Gitxsan village located on the Skeena River between Anspayaxw and Gitanmaax

Sinankxws	Hereditary name from Wilps Hak'w, a Frog Clan house from Kitwanga
Skabek̲	Hereditary name of the Git'tsim'gedimgyat, a Wolf Clan house from Anspayaxw
Ska'wo	Mother of the Children of the Sky; central figure in the Adaawk of Ska'wo
Spagim ganaa'w	Crest of six frogs owned by the House of Hak'w
Spookw	Hereditary name of a Wolf Clan house from Gitanmaax
Stekyoden; Sdigyoodanax	Prominent mountain near New Hazelton BC; central to the Temlaxam Adaawk
Suu 'Wii Gantxw	Hereditary name of Gyetm Maxmagii, a Fireweed Clan house from Gitsegukla
Tax'niibaxw	Adopted name of anthropologist Heather Harris
Temlaxam; T'emlax'aamit	Ancient city on the Skeena River; origin of many Gitxsan, Nisg̲a'a, and Tsimshian houses
Tsi'basaa	Hereditary name of the Git'luuhl'um'hetxwit, a Fireweed Clan house from Anspayaxw
Ts'a'os	Ancient ancestral village; no longer inhabited
Tsihl'nii'din	Creek located north of Anspayaxw
Ts'iiyee	Ancestral warrior and hereditary name of the Git'tsim'gedimgyat, a Wolf Clan house from Anspayaxw
Tsimshian; Ts'msyen; Ts'imsan	Neighbouring and ancestral relative of the Gitxsan; located around the mouth of the Skeena River
Tyendinaga	Mohawk community on the northern shore of Lake Ontario

'Waak	Supernatural baby mountain goat from the Temlaxam Adaawk
Wet'suwet'en	Ancestral neighbours and allies of the Gitxsan along the Bulkley River
'Wii Muugulsxw; 'Wii Mugwilisxw	Hereditary name of the Git'tsim'gedimgyat, a Wolf Clan house from Anspayaxw
Wildim wax	Ancestor referenced in the Adaawk of the Git'luuhl'um'hetxwit
Wilp Aasosxw	No-kill dog sanctuary north of Kispiox, on the Lax'yip known as Naa Dax Deet
Wilps Hak'w	Frog Clan house from Kitwanga
Wilt gallii bax	Ancestral village of the Git'luuhl'um'hetxwit south of Kispiox
Woosimlaxha	Hereditary name of a Fireweed Clan house from Anspayaxw
X̲hliimlax̲ha	Hereditary name of Wilps X̲hliimlax̲ha, a Wolf Clan house from Anspayaxw; once held by Martha Brown
Xsan Seegit	Lax'yip belonging to the Git'tsim'gedimgyat
X̲saxgyoo	Hereditary name of the Git'tsim'gedimgyat, a Wolf Clan house from Anspayaxw
Xsi wis an skit	Name of a creek and the northern territory of the Git'luuhl'um'hetxwit
Xsim Wilaat	Hereditary name of the Git'luuhl'um'hetxwit, a Fireweed Clan house from Anspayaxw; meaning "Lady Echo"
Xsiwis	Hereditary name of Wilps 'Wii K'aax, A Wolf Clan house from Kisgegas; held by Dr. Jane Smith
Yeel	Ancestral warrior and hereditary name in the House of Gitluudaahlxw, a Fireweed Clan house from Anspayaxw

NOTES

Introduction. Lessons from Stand with Wet'suwet'en

1 Guenther, "Property, Dispossession, and State Violence," 81–98.

2 Corntassel and Scow, "Everyday Acts of Resurgence," 55–68.

3 Berg and Seeber, *The Slow Professor*.

4 In this time period, a friendship also formed between Neas-D-Hok and Haxbagwootxw (Ken Harris) around their shared oral histories: "Ken Harris was interested in Walter Wright's version. . . . He said that as part of the Indian way of getting to understand relatives in different areas and of making sure that the myths remain faithful to the original, he lived with Walter Wright for three years from 1936–1939 and that Mr. Wright later lived with Ken's family for six months. They listened to each other's versions of the stories, and it became clear to Ken that Walter Wright's versions were Tsimshian in language and thought, not Gitksan." K.B. Harris and Robinson, *Visitors Who Never Left*, 22.

5 Robinson and Wright, *Men of M'deek*, 17.

6 Beynon and Barbeau, *Temlarh'am*; Barbeau, *The Downfall of Temlaham*, 178–205, 249–53. Barbeau's novel is derived from Beynon's field notes. One of Barbeau's contemporaries, Franz Boas, attributes an origin story about the Sun held among Tsimshian in the early twentieth century to Interior Salish societies such as the Secwépemc, Lower Nlaka'pamux, Syilx, and Ktunaxa peoples, "with no analogue whatever on the North Pacific Coast." This suggests Gyamkian coastal cosmology was always fluid and fusing with other Indigenous cosmologies. For more on this, see Boas, *Tsimshian Mythology*, 113–15, 727–28, 872, 975.

7 In addition to Beynon and Barbeau's work, we draw on several Gitxsan fireweed House accounts for this summary of the Ska'wo oral history. For the House of Gyetm Maxmagii's account, see Gwaans (Olive Ryan), 10–12 June, 15–18 June 1987, B.C.S.C. trial transcript, evidence for Delgamuukw v. The Queen, [1991] 79 D.L.R. (4th) 185, pp. 1003–1519 at 1098–1109 (hereafter cited as Gwaans Testimony). Gwaans had permission from the fireweed Houses of Guxsan and Gwis Gyen to tell this oral history at trial as evidence of their shared origins. We also consulted the fireweed House of Haxbagwootxw's published account in Harris and Robinson, *Visitors Who Never Left*, 17. Finally, Madigaam Gyamk (Neil J. Sterritt) from the fireweed House of Gitluudaahlxw provides a published account in Sterritt, *Mapping My Way Home*, 26–28. We note some discrepancies regarding the names of the grandmother–granddaughter duo and number of children among these Gitxsan sources and between these Gitxsan sources and Barbeau's account.

8 The Ska'wo account is an ancient example of Gitxsan women and girls exercising their legal agency. For more on the legal relationships and obligations held by Gitxsan matriarchs, see Napoleon, "Gitxsan Legal Personhood," 19–32.

9 Beynon and Barbeau, *Temlarh'am*, 14.
10 Gwaans Testimony, 1099.
11 Beynon and Barbeau, *Temlarh'am*, 33.
12 There are two dialects of Gitxsanimx̱, the western downriver (gyeets) and the eastern upriver (gigeenix). We use the eastern upriver gigeenix dialect and rely on the following resources for spellings: Sim'algax̱ Working Group, *Ha'niimagooansxwhum algaxhl Gitksen-Gitksan*; Smith (Xsiwis), *Gitxsanimx̱ Speller*; Smith (Xsiwis), *The Gitxsanimx̱ Teacher*.
13 Smith, *The Gitxsanimx̱ Teacher*, 7.
14 Amawil Hanaak (Laura Forster), personal correspondence, August 2022.
15 For a summary of the case, see Persky, *Delgamuukw*.
16 Neylan, *The Heavens Are Changing*.
17 Harris and Robinson, *Visitors Who Never Left*, 22; 'Wii Muk'willixw (Art Wilson), *Heartbeat of the Earth*.
18 For the importance of Indigenous intellectuals serving as word warriors at the discursive level of engagement with the Canadian state, see Turner, *This Is Not a Peace Pipe*. For the Canadian philosophical inspiration for this Wittgensteinian style of engagement, see Tully, *Public Philosophy in a New Key*.
19 Sterritt, *Mapping My Way Home*, 321.
20 Einstein, *Cosmic Religion*, 43–54.
21 Johnson, "Questions About Questions," 83.
22 See Calls to Justice nos. 1.8 and 7.3 in National Inquiry, *Reclaiming Power and Place*, 1b:173, 1b:188.
23 'Wii Muk'willixw (Art Wilson), *Heartbeat of the Earth*, 32.
24 The intellectual basis of Indigenous legal orders in Canada has been documented by Gordon Christie, John Borrows, and other leading scholars over the past two decades. See, for example, Christie, "Indigenous Legal Theory," 195; Borrows, *Recovering Canada*; Borrows, *Canada's Indigenous Constitution*; Borrows, *Law's Indigenous Ethics*; Friedland and Napoleon, "Gathering the Threads," 16; Lindberg, "Critical Indigenous Legal Theory," 224. For a literature review of the field, see Coyle, "Indigenous Legal Orders in Canada," 1.

Chapter 1. Wilp/House

1 Antgulilbix (Mary Johnson), 27–29 May, 8–10 June 1987, B.C.S.C. trial transcript, evidence for Delgamuukw v. The Queen, [1991] B.C.J. no. 525, 79 D.L.R. (4th) 185, pp. 616–846, 862–1012 at 828 (hereafter cited as Antgulilbix Testimony).
2 See, for example, Galois, "Gitxsan Law and Settler Disorder"; Overstall, "A People of Themselves," forthcoming.
3 For the first published book-length Gitxsan House account of Temlaxam, see Harris and Robinson, *Visitors Who Never Left*. For a commentary on this work, see Grenier, "Esdii Wal," 64.
4 See, for example, Garfield, *The Tsimshian*; Boas, *Tsimshian Mythology*.
5 Robinson and Wright, *Men of M'deek*, 41–42.

6 "It is a movement that carries us beyond success and failure, to a way of being that allows the full spectrum of our life experiences, our hopes and fears, to play itself out within the field of life itself unfolding, flowering in each moment we are fully present with it, for it, and in it." Kabat-Zinn, *Full Catastrophe Living*, 595.
7 National Inquiry, *Reclaiming Power and Place*, 1a:353.
8 For studies on Gitxsan reincarnation, see Mills, "Sacred Land and Coming Back," 309; Mills, "Boundaries of the Self," 81. For a survey of diverse Indigenous accounts of reincarnation, see Mills and Slobodin, *Amerindian Rebirth*.
9 X̲hliimlax̲ha (Martha Brown), 22–23 January 1986 (vol. 4), commissioned evidence for Delgamuukw v. The Queen, [1991] B.C.J. no. 525, 79 D.L.R (4th) 185, 86.
10 Antgulilbix Testimony, 624.
11 Antgulilbix Testimony, 626.
12 Antgulilbix Testimony, 746.
13 Antgulilbix Testimony, 625.
14 Duff, "Contributions of Marius Barbeau," 67–68.
15 Duff, 68.
16 Duff, 68.
17 Duff, *Histories, Territories and Laws*.
18 Duff, 40.
19 Antgulilbix Testimony, 627.
20 Antgulilbix Testimony, 627.
21 Antgulilbix Testimony, 629.
22 Antgulilbix Testimony, 629.
23 Antgulilbix Testimony, 751.
24 Gwaans (Olive Ryan), 10–12 June, 15–18 June 1987, B.C.S.C. trial transcript, evidence for Delgamuukw v. The Queen (1991), 79 D.L.R. (4th) 185, pp. 1003–1519 at 1329.
25 Napoleon, "Raven's Garden," 149. For a recent discussion, see Napoleon, "Gitxsan Legal Personhood," 19–32.
26 Mowatt, "Gwalxyee'enst," 29.
27 For more on these adoption practices, see Harris, "Only Their Skins Change," 114–20.
28 National Inquiry, *Reclaiming Power and Place*, 1a:353.
29 Truth and Reconciliation Commission, *Final Report*, 6:226.
30 Sterritt, *Mapping My Way Home*, 321.
31 Robinson and Martin, *Arts of Engagement*.

Chapter 2. Pdeek/Clan

1 X̲hliimlax̲ha (Martha Brown), 22–23 January 1986 (vol. 4), commissioned evidence for Delgamuukw v. The Queen, [1991] B.C.J. no. 525, 79 D.L.R. (4th) 185, 86 (hereafter cited as X̲hliimlax̲ha Commissioned Evidence).
2 Garfield, *The Tsimshian*, 20.

3 Graeber and Wengrow, *The Dawn of Everything*, 123.

4 For more on the Temlaxam clan origins, see Sterritt, *Mapping My Way Home*, 26–27. For the territorial location, see Antgulilbix (Mary Johnson), 27–29 May, 8–10 June 1987, B.C.S.C. trial transcript, evidence for Delgamuukw v. The Queen, [1991] B.C.J. no. 525, 79 D.L.R. (4th) 185, pp. 616–846, 862–1012 at 664.

5 Harris, "Remembering 10,000 Years of History," 190–96.

6 Barbeau, *Totem Poles of the Gitksan*, 110–11; Cassidy, *From Mountain to Mountain*, 26; Napoleon, "Ayook," 6.

7 Tenimgyet (Art Matthews), 14–18 March, 21 March, 23 March 1988, B.C.S.C. trial transcript, evidence for Delgamuukw v. The Queen, [1991] B.C.J. no. 525, 79 D.L.R. (4th) 216, pp. 4513–4974 at 4777–4778. For commentary on this, see Napoleon, "Ayook," 152–53.

8 Harris, "Only Their Skins Change," 80. On the importance of conceptual and physical mobility to Indigenous legal orders, see Borrows, *Freedom and Indigenous Constitutionalism*.

9 Barbeau and Beynon, "Kispayaks-Laxgibu," field notes, B-F-78, box B6, 1–130 at 11, Marius Barbeau and William Beynon Papers. Canadian Museum of History Archives.

10 Woosimlaxha (Jimmy Williams), "The Origin of the Wolf House of Hawaao," transcribed by William Beynon in 1920, in Marius Barbeau and William Beynon, *Wolf-Clan Invaders from the Northern Plateaux Among the Tsimsyans*, box, 9, f.1, 325–329 at 329.

11 X̲hliimlax̲ha Commissioned Evidence, 84–86.

12 Gitluudaahlxw (Pete Muldoe), 16–20 May, 24–26 May 1988, B.C.S.C. trial transcript, evidence for Delgamuukw v. The Queen, [1991] B.C.J. no. 525, 79 D.L.R. (4th) 185, pp. 6084–6619 at 6116, 6344 (hereafter cited as Gitluudaahlxw Testimony).

13 Madiigam Gyamk (Neil J. Sterritt), 12–16, 19–23, 26–28 September 1988, 11–14 October, 24–26 October 1988, B.C.S.C. trial transcript, 7610 at 8174, evidence for Delgamuukw v. The Queen, [1991] B.C.J. no. 525, 79 D.L.R. (4th) 185, pp. 7610–9048 at 8179–8180. Madiigam Gyamk trial records misspell *Xsan Seegit* as "Ant Gilek." X̲hliimlax̲ha Commissioned Evidence, 100–1; and Gitluudaahlxw Testimony, 6527.

14 Hawaaw (Alice Wilson), sworn affidavit, 25 May 1988, Delgamuukw v. The Queen, B.C.S.C., Smithers Registry No. 0843.

15 For a recorded precedent of clan-based Gitxsan governance addressing a conflict between Houses over a crest, see Napoleon, "Living Together," 45.

16 See, for example, Jang, "How Public Funds Ended Up"; Jang, "Internal Division in Gitxsan First Nation."

17 Mowatt, "Authority Making," 118.

18 Sterritt, *Mapping My Way Home*, 334.

19 For more on this practice, see Napoleon, "Ayook," xi, 120–21, 174, 206, 214–15.

20 Napoleon, 151.

Chapter 3. Lax'yip/Territory

1 See, for example, Sterritt, "25 Years After the Delgamuukw Case."
2 Napoleon, "Tsilhqot'in Law of Consent," 873; Borrows, "The Durability of Terra Nullius," 701; Fraser, "Taking the 'Aboriginal Perspective' Seriously," 21.
3 Our argument for 'wii gyamk generous Gitxsan title as a sovereign right rather than a property right is informed by the analyses of Sanderson and Singh, "Aboriginal Title Property," 417–60. Also see Borrows, "Sovereignty's Alchemy," 537.
4 Antgulilbix (Mary Johnson), 27–29 May, 8–10 June 1987, B.C.S.C. trial transcript, evidence for Delgamuukw v. The Queen, [1991] B.C.J. no. 525, 79 D.L.R. (4th) 185, pp. 616–846, 862–1012 (hereafter cited as Antgulilbix Testimony); Gwaans (Olive Ryan), 10–12 June, 15–18 June 1987, B.C.S.C. trial transcript, evidence for Delgamuukw v. The Queen (1991), 79 D.L.R. (4th) 185, pp. 1003–1519 (hereafter cited as Gwaans Testimony).
5 *T'am Lax amit* is another way Temlaxam is spelt in the trial transcripts. For other accounts of the ancient city, see K.B. Harris and Robinson, *Visitors Who Never Left*; Beynon and Barbeau, *Temlarh'am*; Barbeau, *The Downfall of Temlaham*; Glavin, *A Death Feast in Dimlahamid*.
6 Gwaans Testimony, 1111, 1296; Antgulilbix Testimony, 665.
7 This oral history is also told by Tsimshian Chief Neas-D-Hok (Walter Wright) and correlates with archaeological evidence of a landfall around Seeley Lake.
8 Antgulilbix Testimony, 667–68.
9 There are two one-horned mountain goat adaawk, one told during the dispersal of Antgulilbix's ancestors from Temlaxam, and the other recounting a time in Temlaxam when the one-horned mountain goat feasted the Gitxsan. The latter version is recounted by Gwaans and shared with permission from the closely related fireweed Houses of Guxsan, Hanamuxw, Gwis Gyen, and Antgulilbix. See Gwaans Testimony, 1111.
10 Gwaans Testimony, 1116.
11 Antgulilbix Testimony, 668.
12 Antgulilbix Testimony, 669.
13 Antgulilbix Testimony, 675.
14 Antgulilbix Testimony, 673.
15 Antgulilbix Testimony, 680.
16 The 'Wii Muugilsxw account we draw on here is found in Sterritt, *Mapping My Way Home*, 39–40.
17 Sterritt, 40.
18 Sterritt, 43.
19 Barbeau, *Totem Poles of the Gitksan*, 110.
20 Cassidy, *From Mountain to Mountain*, 18.
21 See, for example, Jang, "How Public Funds Ended Up"; Jang, "Internal Division in Gitxsan First Nation"; Sterritt et al., *Tribal Boundaries in the Nass Watershed.*
22 Antgulilbix Testimony, 800–801.

23 For a record of ancient xsiisxw/compensation law cases among Gitxsan and surrounding Indigenous peoples, see Sterritt at al., *Tribal Boundaries in the Nass Watershed.*

24 Cowichan Tribes v. Attorney General of Canada, 2025 B.C.S.C. 1490 (7 August 2025).

25 Coulthard, *Red Skin, White Skin.*

26 As analyzed in Foucault, *The Courage of Truth*, 269–91.

Chapter 4. Yukxw/Feast

1 Hanamuxw (Joan Ryan), 23 March 1988, B.C.S.C. trial transcript, evidence for Delgamuukw v. The Queen, [1991] B.C.J. no. 525, 79 D.L.R. (4th) 185, pp. 4975–5042 at 5017 (hereafter cited as Hanamuxw Testimony).

2 For seating protocols and a layout sketch of the wilp li'ligit by Tsimshian writer William Beynon, see Anderson and Halpin, *Potlatch at Gitsegukla*, 57–58, 71.

3 For accounts of this tragedy, see 'Wii Muk'willixw (Art Wilson), *Heartbeat of the Earth*, 28; X̲hliimlax̲ha (Martha Brown), 19 September 1985 (vol. 1), 30 October 1985, commissioned evidence for Delgamuukw v. The Queen, [1991] B.C.J. no. 525, 79 D.L.R. (4th) 185 at 14–15.

4 Anderson and Halpin, *Potlatch at Gitsegukla*, 37.

5 For the historical details of Hanamuxw (Fanny Johnson)'s two poles, see Overstall, "A People of Themselves," 35–36.

6 Gwaans (Olive Ryan), 10–12 June, 15–18 June 1987, B.C.S.C. trial transcript, evidence for Delgamuukw v. The Queen (1991), 79 D.L.R. (4th) 185, pp. 1003–1519 at 1064–1072 (hereafter cited as Gwaans Testimony).

7 Gwaans Testimony, 1083–1089.

8 Gwaans Testimony, 1089–1092.

9 Gwaans Testimony, 1498. For more on the commercialization of poles, see Lefroy, "Justice Beyond Legalism."

10 Gwaans Testimony, 1051.

11 Gwaans Testimony, 1162.

12 Hanamuxw Testimony, 5026.

13 Hanamuxw Testimony, 5026.

14 Gwaans Testimony, 1126.

15 Gwaans Testimony, 1129.

16 These estimates are provided in Barbeau, *Totem Poles of the Gitksan*, 112, 189–90.

17 Anderson and Halpin, *Potlatch at Gitsegukla*, 48–50.

18 Barbeau, Beynon, and Williams, "The Origin of the Wolf House of Hawaao," 278–80.

19 Barbeau, *Totem Poles of the Gitksan*, 111.

20 Spinoza, *A Spinoza Reader.*

21 In this regard, scholars are already taking note. See, for example, Napoleon, "Gitxsan Democracy," 195–213; Webber, "Governing Ourselves."

Chapter 5. Sisatxw/Making a New Day

1 See, for example, Smith, "Origin of the Mosquito" and "The Young Chief," in "Placing Gitxsan Stories," 91–93 and 107–8.

2 Barbeau, *The Downfall of Temlaham*, 196.

3 Barbeau, 196.

4 Barbeau, 196.

5 Barbeau, 197. The turn of phrase "sun-lit maturity" is coined by the Chinese science fiction writer Cixin Liu: "Three centuries of drifting alone in the depths of space, an unimaginable life among aliens, the countless tribulations and trials endured in body and spirit—none of these had left any mark on his body. All that was left was maturity, a sunlit maturity, like the swaying stalks of golden wheat behind him." Liu, *Death's End*, 306.

6 Barbeau, 197.

7 Barbeau, 198.

8 Barbeau, 198–99.

9 Robinson and Wright, *Men of M'deek*, 46.

10 Robinson and Wright, 47.

11 Robinson and Wright, 47.

12 Robinson and Wright, 48–50.

13 Barbeau, Beynon, and Williams, "The Origin of the Wolf House of Hawaao," 278–80.

14 Barbeau, *Totem Poles of the Gitksan*, 112.

15 Barbeau, Beynon, and Williams, "The Origin of the Wolf House of Hawaao," 279.

16 Barbeau, Beynon, and Williams, 280.

17 Fasting and bathing are purification rites historically implemented for regaining one's daxgyet. See Harris, "Only Their Skins Change," 24–26.

18 Gwis Gyen (Stanley Williams), 11–18 April, 19–21 April, 26 April 1988, B.C.S.C. commissioned evidence for Delgamuukw v. The Queen, [1991] B.C.J. no. 525, 79 D.L.R. (4th) 185, pp. 1–389 at 178 (hereafter cited as Gwis Gyen Commissioned Evidence).

19 Gwis Gyen Commissioned Evidence, 179.

20 Gwis Gyen Commissioned Evidence, 16.

21 Gwis Gyen Commissioned Evidence, 17.

22 Gwaans (Olive Ryan), 10–12 June, 15–18 June 1987, B.C.S.C. trial transcript, evidence for Delgamuukw v. The Queen (1991), 79 D.L.R. (4th) 185, pp. 1003–1519 at 1255.

23 "Among the Gitksan, according to Luke Fowler, May 24, 1926, devil's club was considered the best of all remedies and all the people knew of it. If it was taken for three or four months broken bones would knit." Smith, *Ethnobotany*, 55.

24 Barbeau, *Totem Poles of the Gitksan*, 111.

25 Beynon, et al., "The Origin of Devil's Club," 82–83; Smith, "Reincarnation (Guuxs witxw)" in "Placing Gitxsan Stories," 74–77. Recent scientific trials have further confirmed the efficacy of the medicine for treating type 2

diabetes, among other ailments. See, for example, Daschbach, "All-Healing Weapon."

26 Gitluudaahlxw (Pete Muldoe), 16–20 May, 24–26 May 1988, B.C.S.C. trial transcript, evidence for Delgamuukw v. The Queen, [1991] B.C.J. no. 525, 79 D.L.R. (4th) 185, pp. 6084–6619 at 6183 (hereafter cited as Gitluudaahlxw Testimony).

27 Gitluudaahlxw Testimony, 6183.

28 Gitluudaahlxw Testimony, 6182.

29 Antgulilbix (Mary Johnson), 27–29 May, 8–10 June 1987, B.C.S.C. trial transcript, evidence for Delgamuukw v. The Queen, [1991] B.C.J. no. 525, 79 D.L.R. (4th) 185, pp. 616–846, 862–1012 at 807 (hereafter cited as Antgulilbix Testimony).

30 Antgulilbix Testimony, 807.

31 Antgulilbix Testimony, 808.

32 Antgulilbix Testimony, 809.

33 Antgulilbix Testimony, 809–810.

34 Camus, *The Myth of Sisyphus*.

35 The notion of "tragic optimism" is coined by the renowned psychiatrist and Nazi concentration camp survivor Dr. Viktor E. Frankl. See Frankl, *Man's Search for Meaning*.

36 For more on sbil naxnox in Tsimshian context, see Marsden, "Adawx," 101–35.

Chapter 6. 'Wii Bil'ust/Star Power

1 Robinson and Wright, *Men of M'deek*, 9, 18, 31, 33–42; Barbeau, *The Downfall of Temlaham*, 178–205, 249–53.

2 Einstein, *Cosmic Religion*, 46.

3 Einstein, 48.

4 Malcolm X claims Spinoza as a Black thinker, the only one to impress him in the Western philosophical tradition. See X, *Autobiography*, 183–84.

5 Einstein, *Cosmic Religion*, 50.

6 Einstein, 51–52.

7 Einstein, 53.

8 Vickers, "Ayaawx," 25.

9 Hanh, *Peace Is Every Step*, 103.

10 Levine and Lang, "Sun."

11 "The stories had traveled in time on the 'Breath of our Grandfathers.' Writing the stories stems from my need to identify the Gitxsan culture and define and protect it because it has the potential to empower." Smith, "Placing Gitxsan Stories," 14.

12 Hanamuxw (Don Ryan), personal correspondence, 7 August 2022.

13 Truth and Reconciliation Commission, *Final Report*, 6:7.

14 In the healthcare sector, the Truth and Reconciliation Commission's Call to Action no. 18 states the following: "We call upon the federal, provincial, and Aboriginal governments to acknowledge that the current state of

Aboriginal health in Canada is a direct result of previous Canadian government policies, including residential schools, and to recognize and implement the health-care rights of Aboriginal people as identified in international law, constitutional law, and under the Treaties." Truth and Reconciliation Commission, *Final Report*, 6:226.

15 Fisher, *Healing the Fragmented Selves*.

16 Smith, "Placing Gitxsan Stories," 110–11.

17 Fisher, *Healing the Fragmented Selves*, 203–6.

18 Fisher, 256–58.

19 Brown, *Atlas of the Heart*, 138–39.

20 Brown, 139. For scholarship that applies Brown's insights on shame in the competitive field of academia, see Berg and Seeber, *The Slow Professor*, 87.

21 Maté with Maté, *The Myth of Normal*.

22 Perry and Winfrey, *What Happened to You?*

23 Maté with Maté, *The Myth of Normal*, 386.

24 Maté with Maté, 388.

25 Maté with Maté, 389.

Chapter 7. Gwil wada/Wilpsta Talents

1 X̲hliimlax̲ha (Martha Brown), 30 October 1985 (vol. 3), commissioned evidence for Delgamuukw v. The Queen, [1991] B.C.J. no. 525, 79 D.L.R. (4th) 185, pp. 1–63 at 39.

2 Gwa'amuuk, "Sharing Sim Algyax," 6.

3 Gwa'amuuk, 7.

4 Gwa'amuuk, 10. For more on the website, see www.gitxsansimalgyax.com.

5 Smith, *Gitxsanimx̲ Speller*; Smith, *The Gitxsanimx̲ Teacher*.

6 Barbeau, *Totem Poles of the Gitksan*, 1.

7 Duff, "Gitksan Totem-Poles," 27.

8 Harris, "Remembering 12,000 Years of History," 352.

9 Sterritt, *Mapping My Way Home*, 30–31.

10 Sterritt, 30–31.

11 Harris, "Remembering 10,000 Years of History," 190–96.

12 Harris, 179.

13 Smith, *Ethnobotany*.

14 Hanamuxw (Joan Ryan), 23 March 1988, B.C.S.C. trial transcript, evidence for Delgamuukw v. The Queen, [1991] B.C.J. no. 525, 79 D.L.R. (4th) 185, pp. 4975–5042 at 4987–4992 (hereafter cited as Hanamuxw [Joan Ryan] Testimony).

15 Hanamuxw (Joan Ryan) Testimony, 5003.

16 Maas Gaak (Don Ryan), "Foreword," iv–v.

17 With theatre director David Diamond, *NO'XYA'* (Our Footprints) toured the country in the late 1980s to raise awareness of the issues at stake in the *Delgamuukw-Gisday'wa* case. For more on this project, see Diamond, *Theatre for Living*, 209–22.

18 See, for example, Hanamuxw (Don Ryan), "Foreword," i; Harris, "Only Their Skins Change," 1; Napoleon, "Ayook," ix.

19 See "Cindy Blackstock, Professor." Blackstock's court battles for the First Nations Child & Family Caring Society and Spirit Bear educational outreach initiatives are especially noteworthy. See, for example, Blackstock and Robinson, *Spirit Bear and Children Make History*; Blackstock, "The United Nations Committee on the Rights of the Child."

20 Hanamuxw (Don Ryan), as cited in Mills, *Eagle Down*, 186–87.

21 For more on Indigenous peoples' contributions to sports in Canada, see Forsyth, *Reclaiming Tom Long Boat*.

Chapter 8. Simgigyet/The Fittest Gitxsan on Earth

1 Anderson and Halpin, *Potlatch at Gitsegukla*, 177–78.

2 Hanamuxw (Don Ryan), personal correspondence, 20 December 2022.

3 Hanamuxw (Don Ryan), personal correspondence, 23 February 2022.

4 Hanamuxw (Don Ryan), personal correspondence, 10 May 2022.

5 Sterritt, *Mapping My Way Home*, 43.

6 Hanamuxw (Joan Ryan), 23 March 1988, B.C.S.C. trial transcript, evidence for Delgamuukw v. The Queen, [1991] B.C.J. no. 525, 79 D.L.R. (4th) 185, pp. 4975–5042 at 5030 (hereafter cited as Hanamuxw Testimony).

7 Hanamuxw (Don Ryan), personal correspondence, 3 April 2022.

8 Hanamuxw (Don Ryan), personal correspondence, 3 April 2022.

9 Gyooksgan makes a strong argument for multimedia resources as supplementary to Gitxsan legal education. See Napoleon, "Did I Break It?," 1.

10 Sterritt, *Mapping My Way Home*, 321.

11 Malii (Glen Williams), 31 May 1988, B.C.S.C. trial transcript, evidence for Delgamuukw v. The Queen, [1991] B.C.J. no. 525, 79 D.L.R. (4th) 185, pp. 6687–6760 at 6739; Malii (Glen Williams), personal correspondence, 3 April 2022.

12 Madiigam Gyamk (Neil J. Sterritt), personal correspondence, 3 April 2022.

13 Hanamuxw Testimony, 5013.

14 Hanamuxw Testimony, 5013.

15 Hanamuxw Testimony, 5005.

16 Hanamuxw Testimony, 5005–6.

17 Gwaans (Olive Ryan), 10–12 June, 15–18 June 1987, B.C.S.C. trial transcript, evidence for Delgamuukw v. The Queen (1991), 79 D.L.R. (4th) 185, pp. 1003–1519 at 1471.

18 Hanamuxw Testimony, 4088.

19 Hanamuxw Testimony, 4088–4098.

20 Hanamuxw Testimony, 5009.

21 Hanamuxw Testimony, 5012.

22 Hanamuxw Testimony, 5010.

23 Hanamuxw Testimony, 5010.

24 Hanamuxw Testimony, 5010.

25 Hanamuxw Testimony, 4977–4981.
26 Hanamuxw Testimony, 4980.
27 Hanamuxw Testimony, 4982.
28 Hanamuxw Testimony, 4983.
29 Hanamuxw (Don Ryan), as cited in Glavin, *A Death Feast in Dimlahamid*, 34.
30 Hanamuxw Testimony, 4983.
31 Hanamuxw Testimony, 5006.
32 Hanamuxw Testimony, 5006–5007.

Chapter 9. Ha gwilii yin/Walking Gently

1 Napoleon, "Ayook," 108. Also see Sterritt et al., *Tribal Boundaries in the Nass Watershed*, 294.
2 See, for example, Barbeau, Beynon, and Brown (Kwiyaihl), "A Peace Ceremony," 164–66. For a recent legal analysis of this g̲awagaani, see Napoleon, "Gitxsan Democracy: On Its Own Terms." For examples of g̲awagaani in Wet'suwet'en context, see Mills, *Eagle Down*, 38, 55, 141–56, 163.
3 Maas Gaak (Don Ryan), "Foreword," in Mills, *Eagle Down*, xi.
4 Maas Gaak (Don Ryan), xi.
5 Wilp Gyetm Maxmagii (Rainbow Person) and Gitsegukla Huwilp, "A Priority Proposal to the Province of British Columbia: Restoring the Gwelx ye'enst Plan for Wilp Gytem Maxmagii and Each of the Gitsegukla Wilp," January 2023, unpublished manuscript in authors' possession.
6 For more on this political notion of inner peace, see Napoleon and Friedland, "Accessing Tully," 208.
7 Napoleon and Friedland, "Accessing Tully," xiii.
8 X̲hliimlax̲ha (Martha Brown), 19 September 1985 (vol. 2), B.C.S.C. trial transcript, evidence for Delgamuukw v. The Queen, [1991] B.C.J. no. 525, 79 D.L.R. (4th) 185, pp. 1–34 at 22 (hereafter cited as X̲hliimlax̲ha Testimony).
9 X̲hliimlax̲ha Testimony, 22.
10 X̲hliimlax̲ha Testimony, 23.
11 X̲hliimlax̲ha Testimony, 22.
12 X̲hliimlax̲ha Testimony, 22.
13 For a Wet'suwet'en law case involving a kus (eagle down) ceremony and shotguns (where the shooting of shotguns is a sign that the parties were going to help each other), see Mills, *Eagle Down*, 149–52.
14 X̲hliimlax̲ha Testimony, 24.
15 X̲hliimlax̲ha Testimony, 24.
16 X̲hliimlax̲ha Testimony, 24.
17 National Inquiry, *Reclaiming Power and Place*, 1a: 353, 339.
18 National Inquiry, 1a:340.
19 National Inquiry, 1a:353.
20 National Inquiry, 1a:353.
21 National Inquiry, 1a:139–140.
22 National Inquiry, 1a:173.

23 National Inquiry, 1a:174. See, for example, Snyder et al., "Gender and Violence," 593; Friedland, *The Wetiko Legal Principles*.

24 "7.3 We call upon all governments and health service providers to support Indigenous-led prevention initiatives in the areas of health and community awareness, including, but not limited to programming: for Indigenous men and boys, related to suicide prevention strategies for youth and adults, related to sexual trafficking awareness and no-barrier exiting, specific to safe and healthy relationships, specific to mental health awareness, related to 2SLGBTQQIA issues and sex positivity." National Inquiry, *Reclaiming Power and Place*, 1b:188. We interpret this call to justice with the findings found under the heading "'We Can't Have Only the Women Heal': Healing Men and Boys," 1b:140–41.

25 National Inquiry, 1b:140–41.

26 We believe our land-based initiative is an especially important Gitxsan legal response in light of Gyooksgan (Val Napoleon)'s analysis that in the National Inquiry's final report, the rights of Indigenous women and girls are placed "outside of Indigenous law and do not derive from within Indigenous legal traditions." She also notes that "while the report speaks to the importance of relationships, the recommendations do not address Indigenous communities or an Indigenous legal response." For more, see Napoleon, "Gitxsan Legal Personhood," 19–32.

27 For more on the role of Indigenous legal orders in addressing crime and incarceration, see Milwaard, *Reconciliation and Indigenous Justice*.

28 'Wii Muk'willixw (Art Wilson), *Heartbeat of the Earth*, 32.

29 Sterritt, *Unbroken*, 241.

30 Antgulilbix (Mary Johnson), 27–29 May, 8–10 June 1987, B.C.S.C. trial transcript, evidence for Delgamuukw v. The Queen, [1991] B.C.J. no. 525, 79 D.L.R. (4th) 185, pp. 616–846, 862–1012 at 750–51 (hereafter cited as Antgulilbix Testimony).

31 Antgulilbix Testimony, 751.

32 Antgulilbix Testimony, 751.

33 Gwis Gyen (Stanley Williams), 11–18 April, 19–21 April, 26 April 1988, B.C.S.C. commissioned evidence for Delgamuukw v. The Queen, [1991] B.C.J. no. 525, 79 D.L.R. (4th) 185, pp. 1–389 at 37.

34 Napoleon, "Ayook," 69–70.

35 National Inquiry, *Reclaiming Power and Place*, 1a:500.

36 National Inquiry, 1b:110.

37 Napoleon, "Demanding More of Ourselves," 227.

38 Napoleon, 232.

39 "We call upon all governments to create specific and long-term funding, available to Indigenous communities and organizations, to create, deliver, and disseminate prevention programs, education, and awareness campaigns designed for Indigenous communities and families related to violence prevention and combatting lateral violence. Core and sustainable funding, as opposed to program funding, must be provided to national and regional Indigenous women's and 2SLGBTQQIA people's organizations." National Inquiry, *Reclaiming Power and Place*, 1b:178.

Epilogue. Sagayt K'i'yhl G̲ag̲oodiit/Unity

1 Sterritt, *Mapping My Way Home*, 322.

2 It was Wet'suwet'en Chief Gisday'wa (Alfred Joseph) along with Delgamuukw (Ken Muldoe) who said it so: "The attempts to quash our laws and extinguish our system have been unsuccessful. Gisday Wa has not been extinguished. . . . If the Canadian legal system has not recognized our ownership and jurisdiction but at the same time not extinguished it, what has been done with it? . . . When this case ends and the package has been unwrapped, it will have to be our ownership and our jurisdiction under our law that is on the table." Chief Gisday'wa (Alfred Joseph) and Delgamuukw (Ken Muldoe), 12 May 1987, B.C.S.C. trial transcript, evidence for Delgamuukw v. The Queen, [1991] B.C.J. no. 525, 79 D.L.R. (4th) 185, pp. 65–141 at 66 (hereafter cited as Delgamuukw and Gisday'wa, Opening Address).

3 Harris, "Remembering 12,000 Years of History."

4 Smith, *The Gitxsanimx̲ Teacher*, 76.

5 Smith, 14–15.

6 Delgamuukw and Gisday'wa, Opening Address, 65.

BIBLIOGRAPHY

Delgamuukw-Gisday'wa Archive

Antgulilbix (Mary Johnson). 27–29 May, 8–10 June 1987, B.C.S.C. trial transcript, evidence for Delgamuukw v. The Queen, [1991] B.C.J. no. 525, 79 D.L.R. (4th) 185, pp. 616–846, 862–1012.

Delgamuukw (Ken Muldoe) and Gisday'wa (Alfred Joseph). 12 May 1987, B.C.S.C. trial transcript, evidence for Delgamuukw v. The Queen, [1991] B.C.J. no. 525, 79 D.L.R. (4th) 185, pp. 65–141.

Gitluudaahlxw (Pete Muldoe). 16–20 May, 24–26 May 1988, B.C.S.C. trial transcript, evidence for Delgamuukw v. The Queen, [1991] B.C.J. no. 525, 79 D.L.R. (4th) 185, pp. 6084–6619.

Gwaans (Olive Ryan). 10–12 June, 15–18 June 1987, B.C.S.C. trial transcript, evidence for Delgamuukw v. The Queen, [1991] 79 D.L.R. (4th) 185, pp. 1003–1519.

Gwis Gyen (Stanley Williams). 11–18 April, 19–21 April, 26 April 1988, B.C.S.C. commissioned evidence for Delgamuukw v. The Queen, [1991] B.C.J. no. 525, 79 D.L.R. (4th) 185, pp. 1–389.

Hawaaw (Alice Wilson). Sworn affidavit, 25 May 1988, Delgamuukw v. The Queen, Supreme Court of British Columbia, Smithers Registry No. 0843.

Hanamuxw (Joan Ryan). 23 March 1988, B.C.S.C. trial transcript, evidence for Delgamuukw v. The Queen, [1991] B.C.J. no. 525, 79 D.L.R. (4th) 185, pp. 4975–5042.

Madiigam Gyamk (Neil J. Sterritt). 12–16 September, 19–23 September, 26–28 September 1988, 11–14 October, 24–26 October 1988, B.C.S.C. trial transcript, evidence for Delgamuukw v. The Queen, [1991] B.C.J. no. 525, 79 D.L.R. (4th) 185, pp. 7610–9048.

Malii (Glen Williams). 31 May 1988, B.C.S.C. trial transcript, evidence for Delgamuukw v. The Queen, [1991] B.C.J. no. 525, 79 D.L.R. (4th) 185, pp. 6687–6760.

Tenimgyet (Art Matthews). 14–18 March, 21 March, 23 March 1988, B.C.S.C. trial transcript, evidence for Delgamuukw v. The Queen, [1991] B.C.J. no. 525, 79 D.L.R. (4th) 216, pp. 4513–4974.

X̱hliimlax̱ha (Martha Brown). 19 September 1985 (vols. 1 and 2), 30 October 1985 to 1 November 1985 (vol. 3), 22–23 January 1986 (vol. 4), commissioned evidence for Delgamuukw v. The Queen, [1991] B.C.J. no. 525, 79 D.L.R. (4th) 185, pp. 1–32, 1–34, 1–63, 1–53.

Published Sources

Gitxsanimx̱ Language Resources

Mathews, Arthur, Jr., and Vera Wale, comps. *Ha'niimagooansxwhum Algax̱hl*

Gitksen-Gitksan: Gitxsenimx̲-Gitxsanimax̲ to English Dictionary. Vol. 1, Learner's Edition. Aboriginal Education Branch, British Columbia Ministry of Education, Gitksan Wet'suwet'en Education Society, School District #88, Sim'algax̲ Working Group, 1998.

Smith, M. Jane (Xsiwis). *Gitxsanimx̲ Speller: Text for Adult Gitxsanimx̲ Class*. Self-published, 2012.

Smith, M. Jane (Xsiwis). *The Gitxsanimx̲ Teacher*. Self-published, 2012.

Secondary Sources

Anderson, Margaret, and Marjorie Halpin, eds. *Potlatch at Gitsegukla: William Beynon's 1945 Field Notebooks*. UBC Press, 2000.

Barbeau, Marius. *The Downfall of Temlaham*. Hurtig Publishers, 1973 [1928].

Barbeau, Marius, and William Beynon. "Kispayaks-Laxgibu." Field notes, B-F-78, box B6, 1-130. Marius Barbeau and William Beynon Papers. Canadian Museum of History Archives, Gatineau, QC.

Barbeau, Marius. *Totem Poles of the Gitksan, Upper Skeena River, British Columbia*. Bulletin No. 61, Anthropological Series No.12, facsimile ed. 1929. Reprint ed., National Museum of Canada and Canada Department of Mines, 1973.

Barbeau, Marius, William Beynon, and Jimmy Williams. "The Origin of the Wolf House of Hawaao." In *Tsimshian Narratives Volume 1: Tricksters, Shamans and Heroes*, edited by John J. Cove and George F. MacDonald. University of Ottawa Press, 1987.

Barbeau, Marius, William Beynon, and John Brown (Kwiyaihl). "A Peace Ceremony Between the Nishga and the Kisgegas." In *Tsimshian Narratives Volume 2: Trade and Warfare*, edited by George F. MacDonald and John J. Cove. University of Ottawa Press, 1987.

Berg, Maggie, and Barbara K. Seeber. *The Slow Professor: Challenging the Culture of Speed in the Academy*. University of Toronto Press, 2016.

Beynon, William, Emma Skatin, Mary Clayton, and Marius Barbeau. "The Origin of Devil's Club." In *Tsimshian Narratives Volume 1: Tricksters, Shamans and Heroes*, edited by John J. Cove and George F. MacDonald. University of Ottawa Press, 1987.

Beynon, William, and Marius Barbeau. "Temlarh'am: The Land of Plenty on the North Pacific Coast." Unpublished manuscript. Canadian Centre for Folk Cultural Studies, Canadian Museum of Civilization, 1950.

Blackstock, Cindy. "The United Nations Committee on the Rights of the Child: Does Its Structure and Working Methods Optimize Efficacy and Promote Child Participation?" *Canadian Journal of Children's Rights* 4, no. 1 (2017): 116–26.

Blackstock, Cindy, and Eddy Robinson. *Spirit Bear and Children Make History*. First Nations Child and Family Caring Society of Ottawa, 2017.

Boas, Franz. *Tsimshian Mythology*. Johnson Reprint Corporation, 1970 [1916].

Borrows, John. *Law's Indigenous Ethics*. University of Toronto Press, 2019.

Borrows, John. *Freedom and Indigenous Constitutionalism*. University of Toronto Press, 2016.

Borrows, John. *Canada's Indigenous Constitution*. University of Toronto Press, 2010.

Borrows, John. "The Durability of Terra Nullius: Tsilhqot'in Nation v British Columbia." *UBC Law Review* 48, no. 3 (2015): 701–42.

Borrows, John. "Sovereignty's Alchemy: An Analysis of Delgamuukw v British Columbia." *Osgoode Hall Law Journal* 37, no. 3 (1999): 537–96.

Borrows, John. *Recovering Canada: The Resurgence of Indigenous Law.* University of Toronto Press, 2002.

Brown, Brené. *Atlas of the Heart: Mapping Meaningful Connection and the Language of Human Experience.* Random House, 2021.

Camus, Albert. *The Myth of Sisyphus and Other Essays.* Translated by Justin O'Brien. Vintage International, 1991.

Cassidy, Maureen. *From Mountain to Mountain: A History of the Gitksan Village of Ans'pa yaxw.* Ans'pa yaxw School Society, 1984.

Christie, Gordon. "Indigenous Legal Theory: Some Initial Considerations." In *Indigenous People and the Law: Comparative and Critical Perspectives,* edited by Benjamin J. Richardson, Shin Imai, and Ken McNeil. Hart, 2009.

"Cindy Blackstock, Professor." School of Social Work, McGill University. Accessed 16 December 2025. https://www.mcgill.ca/socialwork/about/people/faculty/cindy-blackstock.

Corntassel, Jeff, and Mick Scow. "Everyday Acts of Resurgence: Indigenous Approaches to Everydayness in Fatherhood." *New Diversities* 19, no. 2 (2017): 55–68.

Coulthard, Glen Sean. *Red Skin, White Skin: Rejecting the Colonial Politics of Recognition.* University of Minnesota, 2014.

Coyle, Michael. "Indigenous Legal Orders in Canada—A Literature Review." *Law Publications* 92 (2017): 1–36.

Daschbach, Alissa Bronwyn. "All-Healing Weapon: The Value of Oplopanax Horridus Root Bark in the Treatment of Type 2 Diabetes." Master's thesis, Western Washington University, 2019.

Diamond, David. *Theatre for Living: The Art and Science of Community-Based Dialogue.* Trafford, 2007.

Duff, Wilson. "Gitksan Totem-Poles, 1952." *Anthropology in British Columbia* 2 (1952): 21–30.

Duff, Wilson, ed. *Histories, Territories and Laws of the Kitwancool.* Royal BC Museum, 1989 [1959].

Duff, Wilson. "Contributions of Marius Barbeau to West Coast Ethnology." *Anthropologica* 6, no. 1 (1964): 63–96.

Einstein, Albert. *Cosmic Religion with Other Opinions and Aphorisms.* Covici, Friede, 1931.

"Einstein's Equations." Archive Photos, Microsoft Encarta 2008 [DVD]. Microsoft Corporation, 2007.

Fisher, Janina. *Healing the Fragmented Selves of Trauma Survivors: Overcoming Internal Self-Alienation.* Routledge, 2017.

Forsyth, Janice. *Reclaiming Tom Long Boat: Indigenous Self-Determination in Canadian Sport.* University of Regina Press, 2020.

Foucault, Michel. *The Courage of Truth (The Government of Self and Others II): Lectures at the Collége de France 1983–1984*, edited by Frederic Gros. Translated by Graham Burchell. Palgrave Macmillan, 2011.

Frankl, Viktor E. *Man's Search for Meaning*. Beacon Press, 2006.

Friedland, Hadley. *The Wetiko Legal Principles: Cree and Anishinabek Responses to Violence and Victimization*. University of Toronto Press, 2018.

Friedland, Hadley, and Val Napoleon. "Gathering the Threads: Developing a Methodology for Researching and Rebuilding Indigenous Legal Traditions." *Lakehead Law Journal* 1, no. 1 (2015): 16–44.

Galois, R.M. "Gitxsan Law and Settler Disorder: The Skeena 'Uprising' of 1888." In *New Histories for Old: Changing Perspectives on Canada's Native Pasts*, edited by Theodore Binnema and Susan Neylan. UBC Press, 1992.

Garfield, Viola, ed. *The Tsimshian: Their Art and Music*. J.J. Augustin Publisher, 1950.

Glavin, Terry. *A Death Feast in Dimlahamid*. New Star Books, 1998 [1990].

Graeber, David, and David Wengrow. *The Dawn of Everything: A New History of Humanity*. Signal, 2021.

Grenier, Nigel. "Esdii Wal: Gitxsan Law Grounded in Epistemology." *University of Toronto Faculty of Law Review* 76 (2018): 64–91.

Guenther, Lisa. "Property, Dispossession, and State Violence: The Criminalization of Indigenous Resistance in Canada." *Philosophy Today* 67, no. 1 (Winter 2023): 81–98.

Gwa'amuuk, Cheyenne (Morgan). "Sharing Sim Algyax: Creating a User-Friendly Website for Sharing Language Resources." Master's thesis, University of Victoria, 2017.

Hanamuuxw (Don Ryan). "Foreword." In *Gitxsanimx̱ Speller: Text for Adult Gitxsanimx̱ Class*, by M. Jane Smith (Xsiwis). Self-published, 2012.

Hanh, Thich Nhat. *Peace Is Every Step: The Path of Mindfulness in Everyday Life*. Edited by Arnold Kotler. Bantam Books, 1992.

Harland, Fraser. "Taking the 'Aboriginal Perspective' Seriously: The (Mis)use of Indigenous Law in Tsilhqot'in Nation v British Columbia." *Indigenous Law Journal* 16/17, no. 1 (2018): 21.

Harris, Heather. "Only Their Skins Change: Gitksan Social Structure, Kinship, and Genealogy." Master's thesis, University of Alberta, 1994.

Harris, Heather. "Remembering 12,000 Years of History: Oral History, Indigenous Knowledge and Ways of Knowing in Northwestern North America." PhD diss., University of Alberta, 2003.

Harris, Heather. "Remembering 10,000 Years of History: The Origins and Migrations of the Gitksan." In *At a Crossroads: Archaeology and First Peoples in Canada*. SFU Archaeology Press, 2017.

Harris, Kenneth B., in collaboration with Frances M. Robinson. *Visitors Who Never Left: The Origin of the People of Damelahamid*. UBC Press, 1974.

Jang, Trevor. "How Public Funds Ended Up in Hands of Gitxsan Chiefs After Pipeline Nod." *Reveal*, 8 February 2017. https://revealnews.org/article/deal-with-b-c-government-is-bribery-more-or-less-says-prominent-b-c-chief-who-accepted-public-money-in-exchange-for-pipeline-approval/.

Jang, Trevor. "Internal Division in Gitxsan First Nation Raises Questions About Informed Consent for LNG Pipeline." *The Narwhal*, 21 February 2017. https://thenarwhal.ca/internal-division-gitxan-first-nation-raises-questions-about-informed-consent-lng-pipeline/.

Johnson, Rebecca. "Questions about Questions: Law and Film Reflections on the Duty to Learn." *Northern Review* 50 (2020): 83–108.

Kabat-Zinn, Jon. *Full Catastrophe Living: Using the Wisdom of Your Body and Mind to Face Stress, Pain, and Illness*. Bantam Books, 2013 [1990].

Lefroy, Isabelle. "Justice Beyond Legalism: Cultural Appropriation of Totem Poles on the Pacific Northwest Coast." *Quebec Journal of International Law* (December 2019): 67–91.

Levine, Randolph H., and Kenneth R. Lang. "Sun." In Microsoft Encarta 2008 [DVD]. Microsoft Corporation, 2007.

Lindberg, Tracey. "Critical Indigenous Legal Theory Part 1: The Dialogue Within." *Canadian Journal of Women and the Law* 27, no. 2 (2015): 224–47.

Liu, Cixin. *Death's End*. Translated by Ken Liu. Tor Books, 2016 [2010].

Maas Gaak (Don Ryan). "Foreword." In *Delgamuukw: The Supreme Court of Canada Decision on Aboriginal Title*. Greystone Books, 1998.

Maas Gaak (Don Ryan). "Foreword." In *Eagle Down Is Our Law: Witsuwit'en Law, Feasts, and Land Claims* by Antonia Mills. UBC Press, 1994.

Marsden, Susan. "Adawx, Spanaxnox, and the Geopolitics of the Tsimshian." *BC Studies* 135 (2002): 101–35.

Maté, Gabor, with Daniel Maté. *The Myth of Normal: Trauma, Illness and Healing in a Toxic Culture*. Alfred A. Knopf Canada, 2022.

Mills, Antonia. "Sacred Land and Coming Back: How Gitxsan and Witsuwit'en Reincarnation Stretches Western Boundaries." *Canadian Journal of Native Studies* 21, no. 2 (2001): 309–331.

Mills, Antonia. "Gitxsan and Witsuwit'en Experience of the Boundaries of the Self: Body-Bounded or Spirit Bound?" *Religious Studies and Theology* 24, no 2 (2005): 81.

Mills, Antonia. *Eagle Down Is Our Law: Witsuwit'en Law, Feasts, and Land Claims*. UBC Press, 1994.

Mills, Antonia, and Richard Slobodin, eds. *Amerindian Rebirth: Reincarnation Belief Among North American Indians and Inuit*. University of Toronto Press, 1994.

Milwaard, David. *Reconciliation and Indigenous Justice*. Fernwood Publishing, 2022.

Mowatt, Gina Lynn. "Gwalxyee'enst: Love and Refusal as Felt Research with Gitxsan Youth." PhD diss., University of Victoria, 2024.

Mowatt, Morgan. "Authority Making on the River of Mist: Reframing the Indigenous Sovereignty Impasse." PhD diss., University of Victoria, 2023.

Napoleon, Val. "Ayook: Gitksan Legal Order, Law, and Legal Theory." PhD diss., Faculty of Law, University of Victoria, 2009.

Napoleon, Val. "Demanding More of Ourselves: Indigenous Incivility." In *Civic Freedom in an Age of Diversity*, edited by Dimitrios Karmis and Jocelyn Maclure. McGill-Queen's University Press, 2023.

Napoleon, Val. "Did I Break It? Recording Indigenous (Customary) Law." *South African Online Press* (2019): 1–19.

Napoleon, Val. "Gitxsan Democracy: On Its Own Terms." In *Democratic Multiplicity: Perceiving, Enacting, and Integrating Democratic Diversity*, edited by James Tully, Keith Cherry, Fonna Forman, et al. Cambridge University Press, 2022.

Napoleon, Val. "Gitxsan Legal Personhood: Gendered." In *Interrupting the Legal Person*, edited by Austin Sarat. Emerald Group, 2022.

Napoleon, Val. "Indigenous Discourse: Gender, Identity, and Community." In *Indigenous Peoples and the Law*, edited by Ben Richardson, Shin Imai, and Kent McNeil. Hart, 2009.

Napoleon, Val. "Living Together: Gitksan Legal Reasoning as a Foundation for Consent." In *Between Consenting Peoples: Political Community and the Meaning of Consent*, edited by Jeremy Webber and Colin McLeod. UBC Press, 2010.

Napoleon, Val. "Raven's Garden: A Discussion about Aboriginal Sexual Orientation and Transgender Issues." *Canadian Journal of Law and Society* 17, no. 2 (2002): 149–71.

Napoleon, Val. "Tsilhqot'in Law of Consent." *UBC Law Review* 48, no. 3 (2015): 873–901.

Napoleon, Val, and Hadley Friedland. "Accessing Tully: Political Philosophy for the Everyday and the Everyone." In *Freedom and Democracy in an Imperial Context: Dialogues with James Tully*, edited by Robert Nichols and Jakeet Singh. Routledge, 2014.

National Inquiry into Missing and Murdered Indigenous Women and Girls. *Reclaiming Power and Place: The Final Report of the National Inquiry into Missing and Murdered Indigenous Women and Girls*. Vols 1a and 1b. Privy Council Office, 2019.

Neylan, Susan. *The Heavens are Changing: Nineteenth-Century Protestant Missions and Tsimshian Christianity*. McGill-Queen's University Press, 2003.

Overstall, Richard. "A People of Themselves: Some Field Notes on Gitxsan Law." In *Indigenous Intellectual Property: An Interrupted Intergenerational Conversation*, edited by Val Napoleon, Rebecca Johnson, Richard Overstall, and Debra McKenzie. University of Toronto Press, 2024.

Perry, Bruce D., and Oprah Winfrey. *What Happened to You? Conversations on Trauma, Resilience, and Healing*. Flatiron Books, 2021.

Persky, Stan. *Delgamuukw: The Supreme Court of Canada Decision on Aboriginal Title*. Greystone Books, 1998.

Robinson, Dylan, and Keavy Martin, eds. *Arts of Engagement: Taking Aesthetic Action In and Beyond the Truth and Reconciliation Commission of Canada*. Wilfrid Laurier University Press, 2016.

Robinson, Will, as told by Walter Wright (Neas-D-Hok). *Men of M'deek and Wars of M'deek*. Skytone Printing and Graphics, 2003 [1941].

Sanderson, Douglas (Amo Binashii), and Amitpal C. Singh. "Why Is Aboriginal Title Property If It Looks Like Sovereignty?" *Canadian Journal of Law* 34, no. 2 (2021): 417–60.

Smith, Harlan I. *Ethnobotany of the Gitksan Indians of British Columbia*. Canadian Museum of Civilization, 1997 [1925–27].

Smith, M. Jane (Xsiwis). "Placing Gitxsan Stories in Text: Returning the Feathers. Guuxs Mak'am Mik'aax." PhD diss., University of British Columbia, 2004.

Snyder, Emily, Val Napoleon, and John Borrows. "Gender and Violence: Drawing on Indigenous Legal Resources." *UBC Law Review* 48, no 2 (2015): 593–654.

Spinoza, Bendict. *A Spinoza Reader: The Ethics and Other Works*. Edited and translated by Edwin Curley. Princeton University Press, 1994.

Sterritt, Angela. "25 Years After the Delgamuukw Case, the Fight for Land Is More Contentious Than Ever." *CBC News*, 15 November 2022. https://www.cbc.ca/news/canada/british-columbia/delgamuukw-25-years-later-1.6646687.

Sterritt, Angela. *Unbroken: My Fight for Survival, Hope, and Justice for Indigenous Women and Girls*. Greystone Books, 2023.

Sterritt, Neil J. *Mapping My Way Home: A Gitxsan History*. Creekstone Press, 2016.

Sterritt, Neil J., Susan Marsden, Robert Galois, Peter R. Grant, and Richard Overstall. *Tribal Boundaries in the Nass Watershed*. UBC Press, 1998.

Swanky, Tom. *The True Story of Canada's "War" of Extermination on the Pacific Plus the Tsilhqot'in and Other First Nations Resistance*. Dragon Heart Enterprises, 2012.

Tully, James. *Public Philosophy in a New Key*. 2 vols. Cambridge University Press, 2008.

Turner, Dale. *This Is Not a Peace Pipe: Towards a Critical Indigenous Philosophy*. University of Toronto Press, 2006.

Truth and Reconciliation Commission of Canada. *The Final Report of the Truth and Reconciliation Commission of Canada*. Vol. 6, *Canada's Residential Schools: Reconciliation*. McGill-Queen's University Press, 2015.

Umeek (E. Richard Atleo). *Tsawalk: A Nuu-chah-nulth Worldview*. UBC Press, 2004.

Vickers, Patricia June. "Ayaawx (Ts'msyen Ancestral Law): The Power of Transformation." PhD diss., University of Victoria, 2008.

'Wii Muk'willixw (Art Wilson). *Heartbeat of the Earth: A First Nations Artist Records Injustice and Resistance*. New Society Publishers, 1996.

Webber, Jeremy. "Governing Ourselves: Reflections on Reinvigorating Democracy Stimulated by Gitxsan Governance." In *Democratic Multiplicity: Perceiving, Enacting, and Integrating Democratic Diversity*, edited by James Tully, Keith Cherry, Fonna Forman, et al. Cambridge University Press, 2022.

Wickham, Jennifer, Brenda Michell, and Michael Toledano, dirs. *Yintah*. National Film Board of Canada, 2024.

X, Malcolm. *The Autobiography of Malcolm X as told to Alex Haley*. Ballantine Books, 1992.

INDEX

www.ingramcontent.com/pod-product-compliance
Ingram Content Group UK Ltd.
Pitfield, Milton Keynes, MK11 3LW, UK
UKHW040631011026
475846UK00024B/252

9 781772 841558